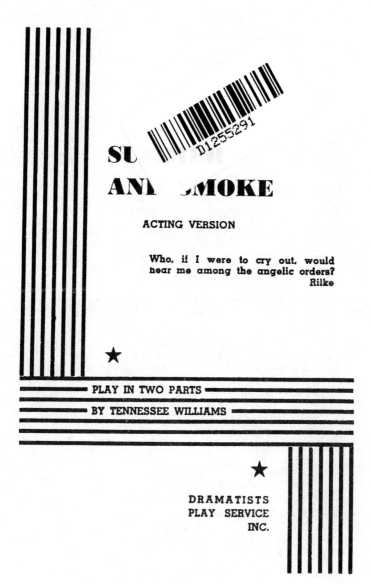

# SUMMER AND SMOKE

### ACTING VERSION

Who, if I were to cry out, would
hear me among the angelic orders?
Rilke

═══ PLAY IN TWO PARTS ═══

═══ BY TENNESSEE WILLIAMS ═══

DRAMATISTS
PLAY SERVICE
INC.

# SUMMER AND SMOKE
Copyright © 1948, 1950, Tennessee Williams
Copyrights © Renewed 1976, 1978, The University of the South

## All Rights Reserved

## SPECIAL NOTE

## ALL TENNESSEE WILLIAMS PLAYS

## SPECIAL MUSIC TAPE

SUMMER AND SMOKE was produced by Margo Jones at the Music Box Theatre, New York City on October 6, 1948. Scenery and lighting by Jo Mielziner; original music and scoring by Paul Bowles; staged by Margo Jones.

## CAST OF CHARACTERS

REV. WINEMILLER
MRS. WINEMILLER
JOHN BUCHANAN, JR.
ALMA WINEMILLER
ROSA GONZALES
NELLIE EWELL
ROGER DOREMUS
DR. JOHN BUCHANAN, SR.
MRS. BASSETT
VERNON
ROSEMARY
DUSTY
GONZALES
ARCHIE KRAMER

## PART I: A SUMMER

SCENE 1. The fountain.
SCENE 2. The doctor's office.
SCENE 3. The rectory interior.
SCENE 4. The rectory interior.
SCENE 5. The doctor's office.
SCENE 6. The rectory interior.
SCENE 7. The arbor.

## PART II: A WINTER

SCENE 1. The rectory and doctor's office.
SCENE 2. The doctor's office.
SCENE 3. The rectory and doctor's office.
SCENE 4. The fountain.
SCENE 5. The doctor's office.
SCENE 6. The fountain.

The entire action of the play takes place in the town of Glorious Hill, Mississippi.

TIME. Turn of the century, through 1916.

3

## AUTHOR'S NOTE ON THE SETTING

[Attention is called to the following note, and nonprofessional directors are reminded that Mr. Williams has here described not only the actual setting he conceived for the production of the play, but the basic over-all mood which is to be established. The stage diagram on p. 28, at the end of the text, will clarify the author's basic requirements, and the specific stage directions as indicated in the text are sufficient for all practical purposes. Essentially, the setting itself is relatively simple; there are no changes in the single setting as here described; lights are centered in one or other of the parts of the single set indicated as described. It need hardly be pointed out that the practical details mentioned throughout should be shown as unobtrusively as possible, a good deal of leeway being allowed to the director in suggesting these realistic matters rather than actually reproducing them.

In one version of this play there is a short prologue which shows John and Alma as young children playing by the fountain. In the present acting version this prologue has been omitted and some material from the prologue introduced into another scene. In case any group is interested in restoring the Prologue, this is included in the reading edition of the play which is published by New Directions, and which may be ordered through your local bookstore. If the Prologue is used it will be noted that certain material used in later scenes in the present edition will not be necessary. The Prologue was omitted primarily because of the difficulty often experienced in securing young children to act the parts—PUBLISHER'S NOTE.]

As the concept of a design grows out of reading a play, I will not do more than indicate what I think are the most essential points.

First of all—*THE SKY*.

There must be a great expanse of sky so that the entire action of the play takes place against it. This is true of interior as well as exterior scenes. In fact, there are no really interior scenes, for the walls are omitted or just barely suggested by certain necessary fragments, such as might be needed to hang a picture or to contain a door-frame.

During the day scenes the sky should be a pure and intense blue (like the sky of Italy as it is so faithfully represented in the religious paintings of the Renaissance) and costumes should be selected to form dramatic color contrasts to this intense blue which the figures stand against. (Color harmonies and other visual effects are tremendously important.)

In the night scenes, the more familiar constellations, such as Orion and the Great Bear and the Pleiades, are clearly projected on the night sky, and above them, splashed across the top of the cyclorama, is the nebulous radiance of the Milky Way. Fleecy cloud forms may also be projected on this cyclorama and made to drift across it. So much for *THE SKY*.

Now we descend to the so-called interior sets of the play. There are two of these "interior" sets, one being the parlor of an Episcopal rectory and the other being the home of a doctor next door [but on the stage separated by a part of the park: see diagram] to the rectory. The architecture of these houses is barely suggested, but is of an American Gothic design of the Victorian era. There are no actual doors or windows or walls. Doors and windows are represented by delicate framework of Gothic design. These frames have strings of ivy clinging to them, the leaves of emerald and amber. Sections of wall are used only where they are functionally required. There should be a fragment of wall in back of the rectory sofa, supporting a romantic landscape in a gilt frame. In the doctor's interior there should be a section of wall to support the chart of anatomy. Chirico has used fragmentary walls and interiors in a very evocative way in his painting called "Conversation among the Ruins." We will deal more specifically with these interiors as we come to them in the course of the play.

Now we come to the main exterior set, which is a promontory in a park or public square in the town of Glorious Hill. Situated on this promontory is a fountain in the form of a stone angel, in a gracefully crouching position with wings lifted and her hands held together to form a cup from which water flows, a public drinking fountain. The stone angel of the fountain should probably be elevated so that it appears in the interior scenes as a symbolic figure (Eternity) brooding over the course of the play. The fountain is backed by massive palmetto leaves like huge spread hands against the sky. *This entire exterior set may (but need not necessarily) be on an upper level, above that of the two fragmentary interiors.* I would like for all three units to form an harmonious whole like one complete picture, rather than three separate ones. An imaginative designer may solve these plastic problems in a variety of ways and should not feel bound by any of my specific suggestions.

There is one more set, a very small exterior representing an arbor, which we will describe when we reach it.

Everything possible should be done to give an unbroken fluid quality to the sequence of scenes. There should be no curtain except for the intermission. The other divisions of the play should be accomplished by changes of lighting.—1948.

## AUTHOR'S DESCRIPTION OF SET INTERIORS

### RECTORY

At stage R. is the Rectory Interior. Down R. in this set is a door frame leading to the rest of the house and to the outside. Up R. a high-backed chair. Up C., against the rear wall, a piano. In front of it, a piano bench. Up L., a small sofa, or love-seat. In L. wall, a window. C. stage a small table, with fringed cover; telephone on L. end of table, a jig-saw puzzle on R. end. At R. of table, another high-backed chair. Down stage C. a fire rail, with an upholstered top.

### FOUNTAIN

The fountain area occupies the C. stage between the Rectory and the Doctor's Office. Up C. the figure of a fountain in the form of a stone angel, on a level with the ramp which runs across the stage representing the town street. On either side of the fountain, stone steps [or simply a rise of ground] leading from the upper level of the ramp down to the stage floor.

Down stage C., a small stone bench, like a park bench, but backless.

### DOCTOR'S OFFICE

The interior representing the Doctor's Office is at stage L. Down stage R., a leather couch. In the up R. wall, a window. Up stage R., a doorway to the street, steps leading from the interior to the street on the level above. Hanging on the wall, up C. R., a chart of human anatomy. Up L., a folding screen. In front of the screen a small table holding a tray with thermos jug and glasses, boxes of pills, medicine bottles, an old microscope, a few doctor's instruments, bicarbonate of soda, gauze and adhesive tape, scissors. C. stage an office desk, holding a phone on the R. end, a skull on the down L. corner, a pen and ink set, pencils, prescription tablet, loose papers. In back of the desk, a leather upholstered swivel chair. In front of the desk, facing C., a straight chair. Down L., a door frame, leading to interior of the doctor's house.

# SUMMER AND SMOKE

## PART I

### SCENE 1

*Before the curtain rises, a band playing a popular selection.*

*The scene is the park in Glorious Hill. It is the evening of July 4th in a year shortly before the first World War. There is a band concert and a display of fireworks in the park. During the scene the light changes from faded sunlight to dusk.*

*As the curtain rises, the* REV. WINEMILLER *is up* R. *standing on the ramp or upper level behind the set, looking off* R. MRS. WINEMILLER *is seated on the ledge at the base of the fountain,* C. *Leaning against the fountain at the top of the steps* L. *is* JOHN BUCHANAN, JR. MRS. WINEMILLER *was a spoiled and selfish girl who evaded the responsibilities of later life by slipping into a state of perverse childishness. She is known as* MR. WINEMILLER'S " *Cross.*" BUCHANAN *is a Promethean figure, brilliantly and restlessly alive in a stagnant society. The excess of power has not yet found a channel. If it remains without one, it will burn him up. At present he is unmarked by the dissipations in which he relieves his demoniac unrest, he has the fresh and shining look of an epic hero.*

WINEMILLER. (*Waving.*) Here we are, Alma!

MRS. WINEMILLER. (*Looking up at* JOHN.) Where is the ice-cream man?

WINEMILLER. (*Coming down two steps to her.*) Mother, hush! (ALMA *appears from* R. WINEMILLER *meets her at top of steps. She sees* JOHN, *stops momentarily, then continues on down steps to bench* C. WINEMILLER, *following* ALMA *down to* R. *of bench.*) I believe they wanted to hear you sing again, Alma.

ALMA. (*Sitting on bench.*) Open my bag, Father. My fingers have

7

frozen stiff! I don't know what came over me—absolute panic! Never, never again, it isn't worth it—the tortures that I go through! (ALMA *had an adult quality as a child and now, in her middle twenties, there is something prematurely spinsterish about her: an excessive propriety and self-consciousness is apparent in her nervous laughter, her voice and gestures belong to years of church entertainments, to the position of hostess in a Rectory. People her own age regard her as rather quaintly and humorously affected. She has grown up mostly in the company of her elders. Her true nature is still hidden even from herself. As* ALMA *comes down steps, R. of fountain,* JOHN *slaps his hands resoundingly together a few times. She catches her breath in a slight laughing sound and crosses quickly down to bench where she sits and fans herself. She is dressed in pale yellow and carries a yellow silk parasol and a hand-bag. Applause of crowd offstage continues.*)

WINEMILLER. (*Anxiously.*) You're having one of your nervous attacks?

ALMA. My heart's beating so! It seemed to be in my throat the whole time I was singing! Was it noticeable, Father?

WINEMILLER. You sang extremely well, Alma. But you know how I feel about this; it was contrary to my wishes and I cannot imagine why you wanted to do it, especially since it seemed to upset you so.

ALMA. I don't see how anyone could object to my singing at a patriotic occasion. If I had just sung well! But I barely got through it. At one point I thought that I wouldn't. The words flew out of my mind. Did you notice the pause?

WINEMILLER. No.

ALMA. Blind panic! They really never came back, but I went on singing—I think I must have been improvising the lyric! (*Looks at* WINEMILLER *as he fumbles through her bag.*) Is there a handkerchief in it?

MRS. WINEMILLER. (*Suddenly, coming down* L.) Where is the ice-cream man?

WINEMILLER. (*Crosses* L. *to her.*) Shh, Mother!

ALMA. (*Rubbing her fingers together.*) Circulation is slowly coming back. . . .

WINEMILLER. (*Crossing down to* R. *end of bench, taking handkerchief out of bag.*) Sit back quietly and take a deep breath, Alma.

ALMA. Yes, my handkerchief—now . . . (*He gives it to her.*)

MRS. WINEMILLER. Where is the ice-cream man?

WINEMILLER. (*Crossing to her down* L., *above bench.*) Mother, there isn't any ice-cream man.

ALMA. No, there isn't any ice-cream man, Mother. But on the way home Mr. Doremus and I will stop by the drug store and pick up a pint of ice cream.

WINEMILLER. Are you intending to stay here?

ALMA. Until the concert is over. I promised Roger I'd wait for him.

WINEMILLER. (*Moving in to her, above bench.*) I suppose you have noticed who is by the fountain?

ALMA. *Shhh!*

WINEMILLER. Hadn't you better wait on a different bench?

ALMA. This is where Roger will meet me.

WINEMILLER. Well, Mother, we'll run along now. (*He gives* ALMA *her bag and starts off up* R. MRS. WINEMILLER *has started vaguely up* L. *He crosses to her.*) This way, this way, Mother! (*Takes her arm and leads her off* R.)

MRS. WINEMILLER (*Calling back in a high childish voice.*) Strawberry, Alma. Chocolate, chocolate and strawberry mixed! Not vanilla!

ALMA. (*Faintly.*) Yes, yes, Mother—vanilla. . . .

MRS. WINEMILLER. (*Furiously.*) I said not vanilla! (*Shouting.*) Strawberry! (JOHN *laughs.*)

WINEMILLER. (*Fiercely, pulling her up off* R.) Mother! We're attracting attention. (*Propels her forcibly off* R. JOHN *laughs.* ALMA *keeps her face averted from him and busies herself arranging her dress.* JOHN *starts down steps* L. *to her and notices a firecracker by lowest step. He bends and picks it up, looks around to see if anyone is observing him, grins, lights it and tosses it toward* ALMA *on bench. When it goes off* [1] *she springs up with a shocked cry, letting parasol drop.*)

JOHN. (*Runs up steps* R. *to top, as if outraged.*) Hey! Hey, you! (*Looks off* R. ALMA *picks up parasol and bag and sinks back weakly on bench.* JOHN *descends steps and comes down* R. *of bench.*) Are you all right?

[1] The explosion of the firecracker can be duplicated by using an ordinary cap as for a cap pistol, which can either be done off-stage or perhaps by Alma under the bench.

9

ALMA. I can't seem to—catch my breath! Who threw it?

JOHN. Some little rascal.

ALMA. Where?

JOHN. He ran away quick when I hollered!

ALMA. There ought to be an ordinance passed in this town forbidding firecrackers.

JOHN. Dad and I treated fifteen kids for burns the last couple of days. (*Puts L. foot up on bench.*) I think you need a little restorative, don't you? (*Takes flask from inside coat pocket.*) Here!

ALMA. What is it?

JOHN. Applejack brandy.

ALMA. No, thank you.

JOHN. Liquid dynamite.

ALMA. I'm sure. (JOHN *laughs and returns it to pocket, taking foot off bench. His steady, smiling look into her face is disconcerting her.* NOTE: *In* MISS ALMA'S *voice and manner there is a delicacy and elegance, a kind of " airiness," which is really natural to her as it is, in a less marked degree, to many Southern girls. Her gestures and mannerisms are a bit exaggerated, but in a graceful way. It is understandable that she might be accused of " putting on airs " and of being " affected " by the other young people of the town. She seems to belong to a more elegant age, such as the 18th Century in France. Out of nervousness and self-consciousness she has a habit of prefacing and concluding her remarks with a little breathless laugh. This will be indicated at points, but should be used more freely than indicated, however, the characterization must never be stressed to the point of making her at all ludicrous in a less than sympathetic way.*) You're—home for the summer? (JOHN *gives an affirmative grunt.*) Summer is not the pleasantest time of year to renew an acquaintance with Glorious Hill—is it? (*She laughs airily.* JOHN *gives an indefinite grunt.*) The Gulf wind has failed us this year, disappointed us dreadfully this summer. We used to be able to rely on the Gulf wind to cool the nights off for us, but this season has been an exceptional season. (*She laughs again. He continues to grin disconcertingly down at her, she shows her discomfiture in flurried gestures.*)

JOHN. (*Slowly.*) Are you—disturbed about something?

ALMA. That firecracker was a shock.

JOHN. You should be over that shock by now.

ALMA. I don't get over shocks quickly.

10

JOHN. I see you don't.

ALMA. You're planning to stay here and take over some of your father's medical practice?

JOHN. I haven't made up my mind about anything yet.

ALMA. I hope so. (JOHN *looks at her.*) We all hope so. Your father's so proud of you and so pleased over your accomplishments. Last time I went in the office, you should have heard him singing your praises. Telling me how you'd graduated *Magna cum Laude* from Johns Hopkins. That's in Boston, isn't it?

JOHN. No, Baltimore. (*Crossing* L. *above bench to* L. *end of it.*)

ALMA. Oh, Baltimore! Baltimore, Maryland. Such a beautiful combination of names! (*Rises, crosses* L. *to him.*) And I have been told that Johns Hopkins is the finest medical college in the world —practically. (JOHN *tries to interrupt, but she goes on.*) It must be a great satisfaction, it must be a real thrill to you, to be standing on the threshold of a career in such a noble profession as I think medicine is. And I seriously believe it is something to which some people are divinely appointed, just appointed by God! (JOHN *crosses* R., *below bench, to up* R.) There is so much suffering in the world it actually makes one sick to think about it, and most of us are so helpless to relieve it, but a physician! Oh, my! (JOHN *turns up to drink at fountain,* ALMA *follows, to his* R.) With his magnificent gifts and training what a joy it must be to know that he is equipped and appointed to bring relief to all of this fearful suffering—and fear! (JOHN *tries to speak.*) And it's an expanding profession—(JOHN *crosses down* L.) it's a profession that is continually widening its horizons. So many diseases have already come under scientific control, but the commencement is just—beginning. (JOHN *again tries to interrupt, she crosses to him down* L., *continuing.*) I mean there is so much more that is yet to be done, such as mental afflictions to be brought under control. . . . And with your father's example to inspire you! Oh, my! (*Crosses and sits on bench.*)

JOHN. (*A whistle of relief and astonishment.*) I didn't know you had so many ideas about the medical profession.

ALMA. Well, I am a great admirer of your father, as well as a patient. It's such a comfort knowing that he's right next door, within arm's reach as it were!

JOHN. Why? Do you have fits?

ALMA. Fits? (*She throws back her head with a peal of gay*

11

*laughter.* JOHN, *too, laughs.*) Why, no, but I do have attacks!—
of nervous heart trouble. Which can be so alarming that I run
straight to your father!

JOHN. At two or three in the morning?

ALMA. Yes, as late as that, even . . . occasionally. He's very patient with me.

JOHN. But does you no good?

ALMA. He always reassures me.

JOHN. Temporarily?

ALMA. Yes . . .

JOHN. Don't you want more than that?

ALMA. What?

JOHN. It's none of my business.

ALMA. What were you going to say?

JOHN. (*Crosses above bench to down* R.) You're Dad's patient.
(*Facing her.*) But I have an idea . . .

ALMA. (*Rising.*) Please go on! (*She laughs.* JOHN *laughs a little.*)
Now you have to go on! (*She crosses to him.*) You can't leave me
up in the air! What were you going to tell me?

JOHN. Only that I suspect you need something more than a little
temporary reassurance.

ALMA. WHY? Why? You think it's more serious than ——?

JOHN. You're swallowing air.

ALMA. I'm what? (*She backs up one step.*)

JOHN. You're swallowing air, Miss Alma.

ALMA. (*Crossing* L. *above bench to* C.) I'm swallowing air?

JOHN. Yes, you swallow air when you laugh or talk. It's a little
trick that hysterical women get into. (*Moves toward her.*)

ALMA. (*Uncertainly, laughs.*) Ha-ha! . . . (*Crossing down to* L.
*of bench.*)

JOHN. You swallow air and it presses on your heart and gives you
palpitations. That isn't serious in itself but it's a symptom of something that is. Shall I tell you frankly? (*Sound of band music off.*)

ALMA. Yes! (*Sits* L. *end of bench.*)

JOHN. (*Crosses down* R. *end of bench, puts* L. *foot up on it.*)
Well, what I think you have is a *doppelganger!* You have a doppelganger and the doppelganger is badly irritated.

ALMA. Oh, my goodness! I have an irritated doppelganger!?
(*Tries to laugh, but is definitely uneasy.*) How awful that sounds!
What exactly *is* it?

JOHN. (*Taking foot off bench, moving away a step.*) It's none of my business. You are not *my* patient.

ALMA. But that's downright wicked of you! To tell me I have something awful-sounding as that, and then refuse to let me know what it is! (*Tries to laugh again, unsuccessfully.*)

JOHN. (*Crosses up* R.) I shouldn't have said anything! I'm not your doctor. . . . (*Leans over, drinks at fountain.*)

ALMA. (*Turning to him.*) Just how did you arrive at this—diagnosis of my case? (JOHN *grins at her—she smiles.*) But of course you're teasing me. Aren't you? (JOHN *starts down stage toward her,* ALMA *turns front.*) There, the Gulf wind is stirring! He's actually moving the leaves of the palmetto! And listen to it complaining. . . . (*As if brought in by this courier from the tropics,* ROSA GONZALES *enters from* R. *She descends steps* R. *of fountain, sees* JOHN. *He watches her, smiling, as she crosses* L. *and ascends halfway up steps* L. *of fountain and turns to look back at him. Her indolent walk produces a sound and an atmosphere like the Gulf wind on the palmettos, a whispering of silk and slight rattle of metallic ornaments. She is dressed in an almost outrageous finery, with lustrous feathers on her hat, greenish blue, a cascade of them. Diamond and emerald earrings.*)

JOHN. (*Sharply.*) Who is that? (ALMA *turns up to look.* ROSA *smiles at* JOHN, *then continues off* L.)

ALMA. (*Turning back.*) I'm surprised that you don't know.

JOHN. (*Crosses to foot of steps* L.) I've been away quite a while.

ALMA. That's the Gonzales girl. . . . Her father's the owner of the gambling casino on Moon Lake. She smiled at you, didn't she?

JOHN. (*Crosses down* L., L. *of bench.*) I thought she did.

ALMA. I hope that you have a strong character.

JOHN. Solid rock.

ALMA. (*Nervously.*) The pyrotechnical display is late in starting.

JOHN. The what?

ALMA. The fireworks.

JOHN. Aw.

ALMA. I suppose you've lost touch with most of your *old* friends here?

JOHN. (*Laconically.*) Yeah.

ALMA. You must make some *new* ones! I belong to a little group that meets every Wednesday. I think you'd enjoy them, too. They're young people with—intellectual interests. . . .

13

JOHN. (*Sadly.*) Aw, I see. . . .

ALMA. You must come!—some time—I'm going to remind you of it. . . .

JOHN. Thanks. (*Crosses in to* L. *end of bench.*) Do you mind if I sit down?

ALMA. (*Rises, moves* R.) Why, certainly not, there's room enough for two! (*She sits* R. *end,* JOHN L. *end of bench.*) Neither of us are—terribly large in diameter! (*Laughs shrilly.*)

A VOICE. (*Off* R.) Good-bye, Nellie!

NELLIE. (*Off* R.) Good-bye!

ALMA. Here comes someone much nicer! One of my adorable little vocal pupils, the youngest and prettiest one with the least gift for music.

JOHN. I know that one. (NELLIE EWELL *enters from* R.—*a girl of sixteen with a radiantly fresh healthy quality.*)

ALMA. (*Extending her hand.*) Hello, there, Nellie dear!

NELLIE. (*Runs down steps* R. *to* R. *end of bench, kneels.*) Oh, Miss Alma, your singing was so beautiful it made me cry. (*Band music offstage ends, there is soft applause.*)

ALMA. It's sweet of you to fib so. I sang terribly.

NELLIE. You're just being modest, Miss Alma. (*Starting to cross up* L.) Hello, Dr. John! (*She comes back down stage,* L. *of bench.*) Dr. John?

JOHN. (*Turning to her.*) Yeah?

NELLIE. That book you gave me is too full of long words.

JOHN. Look 'em up in the dictionary, Nellie.

NELLIE. I did, but you know how dictionaries are. You look up one long word and it gives you another, and you look up that one and it gives you the long word you looked up in the first place. (JOHN *laughs.* NELLIE *starts up steps* L., *calling over her shoulder.*) I'm coming over tomorrow for you to explain it all to me. (*Laughs and runs off* L.)

ALMA. What book is she talking about?

JOHN. A book I gave her—about the facts of nature. She came over to the office and told me her mother wouldn't tell her anything, and she had to know because she'd fallen in love.

ALMA. (*Laughs.*) Why, the precocious little—imp!

JOHN. What sort of a mother has she?

ALMA. Mrs. Ewell's the merry widow of Glorious Hill. They say that she goes to the depot to meet every train in order to make the

14

acquaintance of traveling salesmen. Of course she is ostracized by all but a few of her own type of women in town, which is terribly hard for Nellie. It isn't fair to the child. Father didn't want me to take her as a pupil because of her mother's reputation, but I feel that one has a duty to perform toward children in such—circumstances. . . . And I always say that life is such a mysteriously complicated thing that no one should really presume to judge and condemn the behavior of anyone else! (*There is a faraway " puff " of fireworks and a burst of golden light over their heads. Both look up.*) There goes the first skyrocket! (*A long-drawn " Ahhhhh! " from invisible crowd, off* R. *This effect that will be repeated at intervals during the scene.*) Oh, look at it burst into a million stars! (JOHN *leans way back to look up and allows his knees to spread wide apart so that one of them is in contact with* ALMA'S. *The effect on her is curiously disturbing. The light on cyclorama sky starts to dim and stars appear.*)

JOHN. (*After a moment.*) Do you have a chill?

ALMA. Why, no!—no. Why?

JOHN. You're shaking.

ALMA. Am I?

JOHN. Don't you feel it!

ALMA. I have a touch of malaria lingering on.

JOHN. You have malaria? (*Grins at her.*)

ALMA. Never severely, never really severely. I just have touches of it that come and go. (*Laughs airily.*)

JOHN. Why do you laugh that way? (*With a gentle grin.*)

ALMA. What way? (JOHN *imitates her laugh.* ALMA *laughs again in embarrassment.*)

JOHN. (*Laughing, rises and moves* L., *facing her.*) Yeah. That way.

ALMA. I do declare, you haven't changed in the slightest. It used to delight you to embarrass me, and it still does!

JOHN. I guess I shouldn't tell you this, but I heard an imitation of you at a party.

ALMA. Imitation? Of what?

JOHN. You.

ALMA. I?—I? Why, *what* did they imitate?

JOHN. You singing at a wedding.

ALMA. My voice?

JOHN. Your gestures and facial expression!

15

ALMA. How mystifying!

JOHN. No, I shouldn't have told you. You're upset about it.

ALMA. I am not in the least upset, I am just mystified.

JOHN. Don't you know that you have a reputation for putting on airs a little—for gilding the lily a bit?

ALMA. I have no idea what you are talking about.

JOHN. Well, some people seem to have gotten the idea that you are just a little bit—affected!

ALMA. Well, well, well, well. (*Tries to conceal her hurt.*) That may be so, it may seem so to some people. But since I am innocent of any attempt at affectation, I really don't know what I can do about it.

JOHN. You have a rather fancy way of talking.

ALMA. Have I?

JOHN. " Pyrotechnical display " instead of " fireworks," and that sort of thing.

ALMA. So? (*Rises, facing away* R.)

JOHN. And how about that accent?

ALMA. (*Looks at him.*) Accent? (*She crosses away* R.) This leaves me quite speechless! (*Turns back to him, crossing to above* R. *end of bench.*) I have sometimes been accused of having a put-on accent by people who disapprove of good diction. My father was a Rhodes Scholar at Oxford, and while over there he fell into the natural habit of using the long A where it is correct to use it. (*JOHN sits on bench.*) I suppose I must have picked it up from him, but it's entirely unconscious. Who gave this imitation at this party you spoke of?

JOHN. (*Grinning.*) I don't think she'd want that told.

ALMA. Oh, it was a *she,* then?

JOHN. You don't think a man could do it?

ALMA. No, and I don't think a lady would do it, either! (*Crosses up to base of fountain,* R.)

JOHN. (*Rising, crossing up on a line with her,* L.) I didn't think it would have made you so mad, or I wouldn't have brought it up.

ALMA. Oh, I'm not mad, I'm just mystified and amazed as I always am by unprovoked malice in people. (*Turns away* R. *two steps.*) I don't understand it when it's directed at me—(*Crosses* L. *to former position.*) and I don't understand it when it is directed at anybody else. I just don't understand it—(*Sits on ledge of fountain.*) and perhaps it is better not to understand it. These people

16

who call me affected and give these unkind imitations of me—I wonder if they stop to think that I have had certain difficulties and disadvantages to cope with—which may be partly the cause of these peculiarities of mine—which they find so offensive!

JOHN. (*Who has lit a cigarette, throws match away, moves up steps L., part way.*) Now, Miss Alma, you're making a mountain out of a mole-hill!

ALMA. I wonder if they stop to think that my circumstances are somewhat different from theirs? My father and I have a certain—cross—to bear!

JOHN. What cross?

ALMA. Living next door to us, you should know what cross.

JOHN. Oh—Mrs. Winemiller? (*Sits on steps L.*)

ALMA. She had her breakdown while I was still in high school. And from that time on I have had to manage the rectory and take over the social and household duties that would ordinarily belong to a minister's wife, not his daughter. And that may have made me seem strange to some of my more critical contemporaries. In a way it may have—deprived me of—my youth. . . . (*Another rocket. Another " AHHHHH!" from off R.*)

JOHN. (*Rises, looks up at rocket, turns back to her.*) You ought to go out with young people.

ALMA. I am not a recluse. I don't fly around here and there giving imitations of other people at parties. But I am not a recluse by any manner of means. Being a minister's daughter I have to be more selective than most girls about the—society I keep. But I do go out now and then. . . .

JOHN. I have seen you in the public library and the park—(*Sits on steps L.*) but only two or three times have I seen you out with a boy, and it was always someone like this Roger Doremus.

ALMA. I'm afraid that you and I move in different circles. If I wished to be as outspoken as you are—which is sometimes just an excuse for being rude—I might say that I've yet to see you in the company of a—well, a—reputable young woman. You've heard unfavorable talk about me in your circle of acquaintances, and I've heard equally unpleasant things about you in mine. (*She rises.*) And the pity of it is that you are preparing to be a doctor. You're intending to practice your father's profession here in Glorious Hill. (JOHN *rises angrily, stamping out his cigarette.*) Most of us have no choice but to lead useless lives! But you were born

17

with a silver spoon in your mouth, you with your wonderful gifts and your looks and your charm! (JOHN *crosses down* L.) You were given—surgeon's fingers! You have a chance to serve humanity. Not just to go on enduring for the sake of endurance, but to serve a noble, humanitarian cause, to relieve human suffering. (*Crossing down to him.*) And what do you do about it? Everything that you can to alienate the confidence of nice people, who love and respect your father—(*He turns to her.*) driving your automobile at a reckless speed from one disorderly roadhouse to another! Heaven have mercy! What are you thinking of, John? —Behaving like an overgrown schoolboy who wants to be known as the wildest fellow in town! You know what I call it? I call it a *desecration!* (*She turns from him, crosses to bench, sits, facing away from him. He crosses to her, sits beside her, taking her hand. She springs up from bench.*)

JOHN. You're not going to run off, are you?

ALMA. Singing in public always—always upsets me!—Let go of my hand. (*He holds on to it, grinning up at her.*) Please let go of my hand.

JOHN. Don't run off mad.

ALMA. Let's not make a spectacle of ourselves.

JOHN. Then sit back down. (*Another rocket. Public reacts as before.* ALMA *sits down on bench, he retains her hand.*)

ALMA. You threw that firecracker and started a conversation just in order to tease me as you did as a child. You came to this bench in order to embarrass me and to hurt my feelings with the report of that vicious—imitation! (*She rises, tries to pull away from* JOHN'S *restraining hand.*) No, let go of my hand so I can leave, now. You've succeeded in your purpose. I *was* hurt, I *did* make a fool of myself as you intended! So let me go now!

JOHN. (*Leading her by hand, he draws her in front of him to his* L., *rising from bench.*) You're attracting attention! Don't you know that I really *like* you, Miss Alma?

ALMA. No — you don't. (*Another skyrocket. Glow — and* " *AHHHHH!* ")

JOHN. Sure I do. A lot. (*Crossing above bench to down* R.) Sometimes when I come home late at night I look over at the rectory. I see something white at the window. Could that be you, Miss Alma? Or is it your *doppelganger* looking out of the window that faces my way?

ALMA. (*Laughing a bit, she crosses, sits* L. *end of bench.*) Enough about *doppelganger*—whatever that is!

JOHN. There goes a nice one, Roman candle they call it! (*He runs up steps* R. *to watch and count puffs of light.*) Four—five—six—that's all? No! Seven! (*He laughs.*)

ALMA. (*Vaguely.*) Dear me . . . (*Fans herself.*)

JOHN. (*Comes down to* R. *of her.*) How about going riding? (ROSA GONZALES *appears at top of steps* L., *starts down.*)

ALMA. When?—now?

JOHN. (*Sees* ROSA—*too carelessly.*) Oh—some afternoon.

ALMA. (*Still facing out, unaware of* ROSA.) Would you observe the speed limit?

JOHN. (*Moving up-stage.*) Strictly with you, Miss Alma.

ALMA. Why, then, I'd be glad to—John.

JOHN. (*Picks up hat on base of fountain, his eyes still on* ROSA.) —And wear a hat with a plume!

ALMA. (*Laughs.*) I don't have a hat with a plume!

JOHN. Get one! (*Skyrocket—" AHHHHH!"* ROSA *laughs, moves leisurely off* L. JOHN *follows her, calling back " Good night " to* MISS ALMA, *who turns and sees them together. She sits motionless a moment, facing out.* ROGER DOREMUS *enters from* R., *carrying a French-horn case. A small man, somewhat like a sparrow.*)

ROGER. (*Descending steps* R., *comes down stage to* R. *end of bench.*) Whew! Golly! Moses!—Well, how did it go, Miss Alma? (*Lights on playing area and cyclorama start to dim.*)

ALMA. How did—what—go?

ROGER. (*Annoyed.*) My solo on the French horn?

ALMA. (*Slowly, without thinking.*) —I paid no attention to it. (*Rises slowly.*) —I'll have to hang on your arm—(ROGER *moves down, extends his arm.*) I'm feeling so dizzy! (*A final skyrocket, and " AHHHHH!" They turn up stage and start up steps,* R. *and off* R. *Playing area and cyclorama dim out, skyrockets appear on sky. As* ALMA *and* ROGER *reach end of ramp* R., *the rockets fade out and a light appears on the angel.*) [1]

## END OF SCENE

[1] All props used in the scenes are brought on and off by the actors in blackouts at the beginning and end of each scene, and all doors and windows opened during the scenes, unless closed as a part of the action during the scenes, must be closed in the blackouts.

# PART I

## Scene 2

*The* DOCTOR'S *office.*

ALMA *and* DR. JOHN BUCHANAN, SR., *are present in doctor's office* L. *The* DOCTOR *is sitting back in a swivel chair, above desk, a palm-leaf fan in his hand. A fine looking old man in the best Southern tradition.* ALMA *is standing up* R. *by window. The scene should be rather peculiarly directed. An effect of languor, of gentleness, a very leisurely tempo to create the feeling of the slow summer and of a long-established understanding and tenderness between the two people: a father-daughter kind.*

ALMA. I don't think I will be able to get through the summer.

DOCTOR. (*Glances at her slowly, reflectively with a faint smile.*) You'll get through it, Alma.

ALMA. (*Turning to him.*) How? How, Dr. John?

DOCTOR. One day will come after another and one night will come after another till sooner or later the summer will be all through with, (ALMA *turns back to window.*) and then it will be fall, and you will be saying, " I don't see how I'm going to get through the fall."

ALMA. But even if I survive it, I won't be the same.

DOCTOR. No?

ALMA. I'll be terribly changed in some way.

DOCTOR. What way do you think you'll be changed in?

ALMA. (*Crosses down to below desk,* C.) If I knew that it wouldn't scare me so. (*Leans over desk, to him.*) I wonder if it's noticeable to people? Can people see it in me? (*Sinking into chair, below desk.*) Or do they just think, " Miss Alma's fading this summer "?

DOCTOR. (*Leaning over desk to her.*) Are you in love? (ALMA *turns away.*) Are you in love with someone?

ALMA. Oh, Doctor John!

DOCTOR. Well, *are* you?

ALMA. There *is* someone who wants me to *marry* him.

DOCTOR. (*Sitting back.*) Oh, you've had a proposal!

ALMA. How astonished you sound!

20

DOCTOR. Not a bit in the world! I'm only astonished it hasn't happened sooner!

ALMA. Well, it *has* happened lately. Finally.

DOCTOR. Well, well, well! Miss Alma is going to be married.

ALMA. Don't you dare speak of this!

DOCTOR. Haven't you spoken of it?

ALMA. No! To nobody—but you.

DOCTOR. (*Leaning forward.*) Who's the young man, Miss Alma?

ALMA. —A nice young man, a very nice young man.

DOCTOR. Well, there are several in town. Which one?

ALMA. I doubt that you know him. He's almost a stranger in town. He and his mother came here recently from Meridian, and he is —he is—a very active church-worker. . . .

DOCTOR. A church-worker?

ALMA. Our Sunday School superintendent.

DOCTOR. Ah?

ALMA. He's talented, too, in music—plays the French horn. His name is Roger Doremus!

DOCTOR. Ah . . . (*Averts face to hide his expression, which is both troubled and amused.* ALMA *leans over to judge his facial reaction.*)

ALMA. You *know* him?

DOCTOR. Oh, yes—yes, I know him.

ALMA. What do you think of him?

DOCTOR. Just what you said. He's nice.

ALMA. Yes, he really is—very nice. . . . (*Settles back in her chair.*)

DOCTOR. (*Rises, picks up fan from desk.*) A little bit on the— uh ——

ALMA. (*Leaning forward again.*) What?

DOCTOR. Well —— (*Makes an indefinite gesture. Vaguely.*) But some young men are like that. . . . (*Goes a few steps* R.)

ALMA. Oh . . .

DOCTOR. (*Turns to her.*) However . . .

ALMA. *What?*

DOCTOR. Well—nothing. (*Crosses to window up* R.)

ALMA. No! Please say what you *think!* After all, it's important to me!

DOCTOR. (*Turns to her.*) Is it?

ALMA. What do you mean?

21

DOCTOR. Important?

ALMA. Is *what* important?

DOCTOR. Whatever *you* said was?

ALMA. All I said was that I wanted to know what you think, but you keep—evading the—issue. (DOCTOR *turns to window, fanning himself reflectively.*)

DOCTOR. (*Turns, crosses to chair above desk.*) A little rain would certainly be a relief.

ALMA. That isn't what we were talking about, Dr. John.

DOCTOR. (*Sitting in chair.*) Old men get absent-minded . . .

ALMA. You just don't want to express a candid opinion.

DOCTOR. On what?

ALMA. On this young man.

DOCTOR. I told you I agreed with you.

ALMA. That he's nice, yes! Naturally! That's understood.

DOCTOR. Well, what more do you want me to say about him?

ALMA. (*Rises, crosses to window up* R.) I don't know why we began to talk about him in the first place. (*Turns to him.*) Except that you are the one person in town that I have ever been able to rely on for a kind and honest and understanding discussion of my —problems. . . . This may very well be my last offer of marriage! (*Turns front.*)

DOCTOR. Why do you say that?

ALMA. I am getting along. All of the girls I grew up with have either married or—gone into something else. Well—(*Moving* L. *toward him.*)—to get back to what we were talking about, I *do* like him, I respect him enormously for his—many—good—qualities. He has a responsible position in the Delta Planters' Bank. And Mr. Hutcheson has told Father that they think very well of him there, that he is in line for promotion. He is distantly related to Mr. Hutcheson. (DOCTOR *turns front.*) In fact, not so distantly. His mother was Mr. Hutcheson's mother's first cousin. They think very well of him there and of course the family connection won't do him any harm, either.

DOCTOR. He strikes me as the sort of young man who would get along very well in the banking profession.

ALMA. Then what is your specific objection to him?

DOCTOR. (*Turns on her.*) What is *yours*?

ALMA. I have none!

DOCTOR. Then what the hell are we talking about, Miss Alma—

(*Rises.*)—if you'll excuse the emphasis? (ALMA *crosses down to chair below desk, sits. He puts his hands on desk, leans toward her.*) I've never known anybody as God-damn touchy as you are!

ALMA. I am sorry that I have exasperated you to the point of profanity. (DOCTOR *straightens up.*) My objection to him is just that I don't love him and cannot imagine myself ——

DOCTOR. (*Leaning over desk again.*) In bed with him?

ALMA (*Rises hastily, crosses* R. *to couch.*) Dr. John!

DOCTOR. (*Crossing down on a line with her.*) Well?

ALMA. (*Sits down-stage end of couch.*) Yes.—I suppose that's it!

DOCTOR. Well, why didn't you come out and say so? Instead of all this beating around the bush!

ALMA. But suppose I got left high and dry? With no one, nobody!

DOCTOR. (*Crossing* L. *and up above desk to* L. *of it.*) Well—you could go to New Orleans as your aunt did and have a mysteriously colorful career on the old side of town.

ALMA. What an unkind thing to say!

DOCTOR. (*Sits in chair above desk.*) Well, my head is spinning!

ALMA. (*Rises, crosses to him on his* R., *puts arms around his shoulders. He pats her hand.*) You won't take care of yourself. Shall I go now? I shouldn't have bothered you. I wouldn't have, but I saw you sitting alone in here, so I—dropped in. (*Crosses down* L. *toward exit.*)

DOCTOR. I thought you wanted to ask my advice about something?

ALMA. You had nothing to say.

DOCTOR. I have this to say, Alma. (*Indicates for her to sit in chair below desk. She does.*) You've got to ask yourself whether or not the sexual side of marriage means anything to you. A gentlemanly fellow, abstemious and easy-going, is all some women look for. On the other hand there are some women who want to love and be loved with physical passion. (ALMA *looks slowly and gravely away.*) Which are you, Miss Alma?

ALMA. I believe in the possibility of a deep love between a man and a woman.

DOCTOR. Good! A physical love?

ALMA. With me it could not be based on physical passion. I think the very term is somewhat unpleasant.

DOCTOR. Forgive me for using it. (*Smiles a bit wearily.*)

ALMA. But, naturally, marriage leads to contacts—embraces?

DOCTOR. Yes?

23

ALMA. And I don't see how I could ever with Roger. (*Turns and looks directly at him.*) It even offends me when he touches my hand—in spite of all the respect that I do have for him, and even affection. . . .

DOCTOR. Has anyone else ever touched you—(ALMA *turns away.*) —I mean your hand—without creating this—distasteful feeling?

ALMA. Yes, I'm not a cold person . . . (*Voice offstage:* " JOHNNY, JOHNNY!" ALMA *rises, crosses to window up* R.) Where's—where's Johnny? I haven't seen him lately. Is he out of town?

DOCTOR. (*Writing on prescription pad.*) You're not the only young lady who's asked me that.

ALMA. That doesn't answer my question.

DOCTOR. The last I heard he was taking part in what is called a " floating crap game."

ALMA. When do you expect him back?

DOCTOR. When he has lost his shirt, socks, tie, and the belt to his trousers.

ALMA. (*Moving* L. *toward him.*) When he comes back—I wish you'd remind him of something. A month ago he said he would take me riding some afternoon in his automobile, but he seemed to forget all about it.

DOCTOR. (*Turns to her.*) I'm afraid you'll have to remind him of it yourself. When he comes back, *if* the no-good whelp comes back, he'll find his belongings moved to the Alhambra Hotel. There is no place in the medical profession for wasters and drunkards and lechers, and there is no place in my house for wasters, drunkards and lechers.

ALMA. Why do you say lechers?

DOCTOR. (*Turning front.*) He spends his nights at Gonzales' place on the Lake. He isn't fit for you to associate with, as your father told you a long time ago.

ALMA. (*Crosses above him, to his* L., *her hands on his shoulders.*) You've got to be patient, because he's young and confused. We've all of us got to be patient. At least till the end of summer. If we can go that far, we can go much further, and somewhere, some time—there must be some revelation, the visit of some angel to straighten things out. (*She kisses top of* DOCTOR'S *head.*) Goodbye, I'm going now. (*Starts out* L. JOHN *enters, door up* R.) John!

JOHN. Hello, Miss Alma. (*Turns to* DOCTOR, *who greets him with a stony look.*) Dad. (*Turns away* R.)

ALMA. Don't be too severe with him!

DOCTOR. Excuse us, Miss Alma. (ALMA *exits* L. JOHN *starts off* L.) You'll find your things at the Alhambra Hotel.

JOHN. (*Turns up to him.*) If that's how you want it. (*Starts out and up steps.*)

DOCTOR. (*Rising.*) John! (JOHN *returns to room again.*) Go upstairs and wash and shave and put on a clean shirt of mine—I'll have the colored boy get your things from the Alhambra.

JOHN. Okay, if that's the way you want it. (*Hastily crosses* L. *and out.*)

DOCTOR. (*Looking after him, supporting himself on desk.*) You— you infernal whelp, you! (*Blacked in* DOCTOR'S *office. Light up on angel.*)


# PART I

## SCENE 3

*Rectory interior lighted.*

MRS. WINEMILLER *rushes onto rectory area through the Gothic door frame* R. *She crosses* L. *to love-seat, sits, opens her parasol, and takes out a fancy white plumed hat. Drops her parasol, rises, turns up stage as though to a mirror, starts to put on hat. Phone rings. Startled, she turns to it. It rings again. Hurriedly she crosses* R. *and conceals hat on floor behind table, then scurries back and sits on love-seat. Phone rings again.* ALMA *enters from* R. *and moves to above up* L. *end of table. Picks up phone.*

ALMA. (*Into phone.*) Hello.—Yes, Mr. Gillam. . . . She did? (*Turns and looks at her mother.*) Are you sure? . . . How shocking! (MRS. WINEMILLER *rises, picks up hat and comes down to sit on* R. *end of fire rail, facing* ALMA.) Thank you, Mr. Gillam —(MRS. WINEMILLER *deliberately puts on hat.*) the hat is here. (ALMA *crosses up* L. *to pick up parasol.* WINEMILLER *enters from* R., *distractedly, sees* MRS. WINEMILLER.)

WINEMILLER. (*Crosses* L. *above table to* ALMA.) Alma! Alma, your mother ——!

ALMA. I know, Father, Mr. Gillam just called. He told me she

25

picked up a white plumed hat and he pretended not to notice in order to save you the embarrassment, so I just let him charge it to us.

WINEMILLER. That hat looks much too expensive.

ALMA. It's fourteen dollars. You pay six of it, Father, and I'll pay eight. (*She hands him parasol.*)

WINEMILLER. What an insufferable cross we have to bear! (*Carrying parasol, he crosses down R. and exits R. As he exits, MRS. WINEMILLER rises, clutching hat, moves R. ALMA crosses to her, and taking her by arm seats her in chair R. of table.*)

ALMA. Now I have a thousand and one things to do before my club meeting tonight, so you work quietly on your picture puzzle or I shall take the hat back, plume and all. (*Crosses to above table, C.*)

MRS. WINEMILLER. (*Throws a piece of jig-saw puzzle, which is on table, to floor, up-stage.*) The pieces don't fit! (ALMA *picks up piece of puzzle and replaces it.* MRS. WINEMILLER *attempts to throw another piece, but* ALMA *restrains her.*) Don't fit! (ALMA *moves to phone, picks it up, then slowly puts it down again. Finally, summoning her courage, picks it up again and unhooks receiver.*)

ALMA. (*Into phone.*) Elm 362 —— (JOHN's *phone rings. Office interior is lighted.* JOHN *enters the office from L., a glass in each hand, mixing a bromo as he goes. Crosses to above desk, drinks mixture, puts glasses on desk, picks up phone and sits on R. arm of chair behind desk.*)

JOHN. (*Answering.*) Hello?

ALMA. (*Laughs.*) John!

JOHN. Miss Alma?

ALMA. (*Laughs.*) You recognized my voice?

JOHN. I recognized your laugh.

ALMA. (*Laughs.*) Ha-ha! How are you, you stranger, you!

JOHN. I'm pretty well, Miss Alma. How're you doing?

ALMA. Surviving, just surviving! Isn't it fearful!

JOHN. Uh-huh.

ALMA. You seem unusually laconic. Or perhaps I should say more than usually laconic.

JOHN. I had a big night and I'm just recovering from it.

ALMA. Well, sir, I have a bone to pick with you!

JOHN. What's that, Miss Alma?

26

ALMA. The time of our last conversation on the Fourth of July, you said you were going to take me riding in your automobile.

JOHN. Aw. Did I say that?

ALMA. Yes indeed you did, sir! And all these hot afternoons I've been breathlessly waiting and hoping that you would remember that promise. (*Laughs.*) But now I know how insincere you are. Time and again the four-wheeled phenomenon flashes by the rectory, and I have yet to put my—my quaking foot in it. (*Laughs.*)

MRS. WINEMILLER. (*Mocking* ALMA.) My quaking foot in it!

ALMA. Mother! Shhhh!

JOHN. (*Rises, moves down, sits* R. *end of desk.*) What was that, Miss Alma? I didn't understand you?

ALMA. I was just reprimanding you, sir! Castigating you verbally! Ha-ha!

MRS. WINEMILLER. (*Grimacing.*) Ha-ha! (ALMA *turns to her mother, hushing her.*)

JOHN. What about, Miss Alma?

ALMA. Never mind. I know how busy you are!—(MRS. WINEMILLER *giggles.*) Mother, hush, please!

JOHN. I'm afraid we have a bad connection.

ALMA. I hate telephones. I don't know why, but they always make me laugh as if someone were poking me in the ribs! (*Laughs.*) I swear to goodness they do!

JOHN. Why don't you just go to your window and I'll go to mine, and we can holler across?

ALMA. The yard's so wide I'm afraid it would crack my voice! And I've got to sing at somebody's wedding tomorrow.

JOHN. You're going to sing at a wedding?

ALMA. Yes. "The Voice That Breathed O'er Eden." (*Laughs.*) And I'm as hoarse as a frog!

JOHN. Better come over and let me give you a gargle.

ALMA. Nasty gargles—I hate them!

MRS. WINEMILLER. (*Mocking.*) Nasty gargles—I hate them!

ALMA. Mother, shhh!—please! As you no doubt have gathered, there is some interference at this end of the line! What I wanted to say is—you remember my mentioning that little club I belong to?

JOHN. Aw! Aw, yes! Those intellectual meetings!

ALMA. Oh, now, don't call it that. It's just a little informal gath-

27

ering every Wednesday, and we talk about the new books and read things out loud to each other!

JOHN. Serve any refreshments?

ALMA. Yes, we serve refreshments!

JOHN. Any liquid refreshments?

ALMA. Both liquid and solid refreshments.

JOHN. Is this an invitation?

ALMA. Didn't I promise I'd ask you? It's going to be tonight!— at eight at my house, at the rectory, so all you'll have to do is cross the yard!

JOHN. I'll try to make it, Miss Alma.

ALMA. Don't say try as if it required some Herculean effort! All you have to do is ——

JOHN. Cross the yard! (*Rises, crosses up above desk, faces down.*) Uh-huh—reserve me a seat by the punch bowl.

ALMA. That gives me an idea! We *will* have punch, fruit punch, with claret in it. Do you like claret?

JOHN. I just dote on claret.

ALMA. (*Laughs.*) Now you're being sarcastic!

JOHN. Excuse me, Miss Alma, but Dad's got to use this phone.

ALMA. I won't hang up till you've said you'll come without fail!

JOHN. I'll be there, Miss Alma. You can count on it.

ALMA. —Au revoir, then! Until eight.

JOHN. G'bye, Miss Alma. (*With a quizzical look, he hangs up phone, picks up the two glasses and exits* L. *Lights in* DOCTOR'S *office dim out to black.*)

MRS. WINEMILLER. (*As* ALMA *hangs up phone, she rises and waltzes, mocking,* L. *below table to up* L.) Alma's in love—in love!

ALMA. (*Sharply.*) Mother, you are wearing out my patience! (*Crossing to her.*) Now I am expecting another music pupil and I have to make preparations for the club meeting, so I suggest that you —— (NELLIE *rings doorbell off* R.) Will you go to your room? (MRS. WINEMILLER *reluctantly crosses* R. *to front of chair* R. *of table, then sits. Doorbell rings again.* ALMA *crosses* R. *to door.*) Yes, Nellie, coming, Nellie! (*Crossing back to* R. *of* MRS. WINEMILLER.) All right, stay down here then. But keep your attention on your picture puzzle or there will be no ice-cream for you after supper. (MRS. WINEMILLER *starts working feverishly on puzzle.* ALMA *crosses to* R. *and off. Offstage:*) Hello, Nellie. (NEL-

LIE *runs in from* R., *wildly excited over something. Runs below table to love-seat up* L., *throws herself on it on her hands and knees, burying her head in sofa.*)

NELLIE. Oh, Miss Alma! (*Wags her head mysteriously from side to side.*)

ALMA. (*Who has followed her in, down* R.) What is it, Nellie? Has something happened at home? (NELLIE *continues mysterious wagging and giggling.* ALMA *crosses below table up to* NELLIE.) Oh, now, Nellie, stop that! Whatever it is, it can't be *that* important!

NELLIE. (*Straightens up, moves around on love-seat to face* ALMA, *then suddenly blurts out.*) Miss Alma, haven't you ever had—crushes?

ALMA. (*A little above* L. *end of table.*) What?

NELLIE. Crushes?

ALMA. Yes—I suppose I have.

NELLIE. Did you know that I had a crush on *you*, Miss Alma?

ALMA. No, Nellie.

NELLIE. Why do you think that I took singing lessons?

ALMA. I supposed it was because you wished to develop your voice.

NELLIE. (*Cutting in.*) Oh, you know, and I know, I never had any voice. I had a crush on you, though. Those were the days when I had crushes on girls. Those days are all over—(*Spreads her legs out, beating on floor with her heels.*) now I have crushes on boys. (*Rises, crosses to* ALMA.) Oh, Miss Alma, you know about Mother, how I was brought up so nobody nice except you would have anything to do with us—Mother meeting the trains to pick up the travelling salesmen—(*Crossing* L. *two steps.*) and bringing them home to drink and play poker—all of them acting like pigs, pigs, pigs! (*Emphasizes this by waving hands up and down.* MRS. WINEMILLER *mimics her gestures and words: "Pigs, pigs, pigs!"* ALMA *restrains her.* NELLIE *crosses* R. *to* ALMA.) Well, I thought I'd always hate men. Loathe and despise them. But last night —— Oh! (*Throws herself on love-seat, face down.*)

ALMA. (*Moving up toward piano.*) Hadn't we better run over some scales until you are feeling calmer?

NELLIE. (*Sitting up.*) I'd heard them downstairs for hours but didn't know who it was—I'd fallen asleep—when all of a sudden my door banged open. He'd thought it was the bathroom! (*Puts head down again.* MRS. WINEMILLER *giggles.*)

ALMA. (*Turning down.*) Nellie, I'm not sure I want to hear any more of this story.

NELLIE. (*Peering up at* ALMA *from her prone position.*) Guess who it was?

ALMA. I couldn't possibly guess.

NELLIE. Someone you know. Someone I've seen you with.

ALMA. Who?

NELLIE. (*Sits up on love-seat, facing* ALMA.) The wonderfullest person in all the big wide world! When he saw it was me he came and sat down on the bed and held my hand and we talked and talked until Mother came up to see what had happened to him. You should have heard him bawl her out. Oh, he laid the law down! He said she ought to send me off to a girls' school because she wasn't fit to bring up a daughter! Then she started to bawl him out. You're a fine one to talk, she said, you're not fit to call yourself a doctor!

ALMA. John Buchanan?

NELLIE. Yes, of course, Dr. Johnny.

ALMA. Was—with—your—mother?

NELLIE. Oh, he wasn't her beau! He had a girl with him, and Mother had somebody else!

ALMA. Who—did—he—have?

NELLIE. Oh, some loud tacky thing with a Z in her name!

ALMA. Gonzales? Rosa Gonzales?

NELLIE. Yes, that was it! But him! Oh, Miss Alma. He's the *wonderfullest* person that I ——

ALMA. (*Crossing* L. *toward* NELLIE.) Your mother was right! He isn't fit to call himself a doctor! I hate to disillusion you, but this wonderfullest person is pitiably weak. (*Someone calls "Johnny! Johnny!" outside, off* L.)

NELLIE. (*Rises, goes to window* L., *opens it, looks out.*) Someone is calling him now!

ALMA. (*Crosses* R. *to above table.*) Yes, these people who shout his name in front of his house are of such a character that the old doctor cannot permit them to come inside the door. (*Moves slowly* L. *to* R. *of* NELLIE.) And when they have brought him home at night, left him sprawling on the front steps, sometimes at daybreak—it takes two people, his father and the old cook, one pushing and one pulling, to get him upstairs. All the gifts of the gods were showered on him—(*Call of "Johnny!" is repeated off* L.)

30

but all he cares about is indulging his senses! (*"Johnny!" comes again, off* L.)

NELLIE. (*Leaning out of window.*) Here he comes down the steps! Look at him jump!

ALMA. Oh.

NELLIE. Over the banisters. Ha-ha.

ALMA. (*Crosses* R. *to above table.*) Nellie, don't lean out the window and have us caught spying.

MRS. WINEMILLER. (*Suddenly.*) Show Nellie how *you* spy on him! (NELLIE *turns from window and looks at her, closes window.*) Oh, she's a good one at spying. She stands behind the curtain and peeks around it, and ——

ALMA. (*Crosses to above* MRS. WINEMILLER *to restrain her, frantically.*) Mother!

MRS. WINEMILLER. She spies on him. Whenever he comes in at night she rushes downstairs to watch him out of this window!

ALMA. (*Moving to* R. *of* MRS. WINEMILLER, *her hands on her mother's shoulders.*) Be still!

MRS. WINEMILLER. (*Overlapping.*) She called him just now and had a fit on the telephone! (*Rises, starts to cross* L.) Alma's in love—Alma's in love!

ALMA. (*Seizes her mother by shoulders and forcibly pushes her down onto fire-rail,* R. *end.*) Mother, be still! (*Pause, as she regains control of herself.*) Nellie, Nellie, please go.

NELLIE. (*Crossing* R., *above table, to down* R.) All right, Miss Alma, I'm going. Good night, Mrs. Winemiller! (*Goes out* R. ALMA *follows her off. Door slam off* R. ALMA *returns swiftly.*)

ALMA. (*Crosses to* C., *below table, above* MRS. WINEMILLER.) If ever I hear you say such a thing again, if ever you dare to repeat such a thing in my presence or anybody else's—then it will be the last straw! (*Crosses up above table, to* L. *end of it.*) You understand me? Yes, you understand me! You act like a child, but you have the devil in you. And God will punish you—yes! I'll punish you, too. I'll take your cigarettes from you and give you no more. I'll give you no ice-cream, either. (*Crosses down, down* L. *end of table.*) Because I'm tired of your malice. Yes, I'm tired of your malice and your self-indulgence. People wonder why I'm tied down here! They pity me—think of me as an old maid already! I'm young. Still young! It's you—it's you, you've taken my youth away from me! (*Crosses two steps up* L.) I wouldn't say that—I'd try not even to think it—(*Turns, comes down stage.*) if you were just kind, just simple! But I could spread my life out like a rug for you to step on and you'd step on it, and not even say "Thank you, Alma!" Which is what you've done always—and now you dare to tell a disgusting lie about me—in front of that girl!

MRS. WINEMILLER. Don't you think I hear you go to the window at night to watch him come in and ——?

ALMA. (*Reaching for plumed hat.*) Give me that plumed hat, Mother! It goes back now, it goes back!

MRS. WINEMILLER. *Fight! Fight!* (ALMA *snatches at hat.* MRS. WINEMILLER *snatches, too. The hat is torn between them.* MRS. WINEMILLER *retains hat. Plume comes loose in* ALMA'S *hand. She stares at it a moment with a shocked expression.*)

ALMA. (*Sincerely.*) Heaven have mercy upon us! (*Lights in rectory dim out to black. Special spot comes up on angel.*)

## END OF SCENE

(NOTE: All people concerned in the following scene, carrying fans, take their places on stage in the blackout. ROGER carries on the minute book to hand to ALMA in the black.)

## PART I

### SCENE 4

*Lights dim up to reveal rectory interior.*

*The meeting is in progress, having just opened with the reading of the minutes by* ALMA. *She stands up* C., *between piano and love-seat, and the others of them, including* ROGER, *seated on* L. *end of love-seat, a willowy younger man with Byronic locks,* VERNON, *sitting in chair* R. *of table. A widow,* MRS. BASSETT, *and* ROSEMARY, *the Public Librarian, a wistful older girl with a long neck and thick-lensed glasses, are seated side by side on piano bench,* MRS. BASSETT *on* R. *end.*

ALMA. (*Reading.*) "Our last meeting which fell on July Fourteenth ——"

MRS. BASSETT. Bastille Day!

ALMA. Pardon me?

MRS. BASSETT. It fell on Bastille Day! But, honey, that was the meeting before last.

ALMA. (*Consulting minute-book.*) You're perfectly right. (*Laughs.*) I seem to be on the wrong page —— (*Some papers from her book flutter to the floor.*)

MRS. BASSETT. Butter-fingers? (ROGER *and* VERNON *both rise to pick them up, but* ROGER *recovers them, and hands them back to* ALMA.)

ALMA. Thank you, Roger—Vernon. (ROGER *and* VERNON *resume their seats.* ALMA *looks at book again.*) Here we are! July twenty-fifth! Correct?

MRS. BASSETT. Correct!

ALMA. (*Continuing.*) " It was debated whether or not we ought to suspend operations for the remainder of the summer, as the departure of several members engaged in the teaching profession for their summer vacations ——"

MRS. BASSETT. Lucky people!

ALMA. "—had substantially contracted our little circle."

MRS. BASSETT. —" Decimated our ranks! " (*Doorbell rings off* R.)

ALMA. (*With agitation.*) Is that—is that—the doorbell?

MRS. BASSETT. It sure did sound like it to me.

ALMA. Excuse me a moment. (*Hands minute-book to* ROGER, *starts* R. *to door.*) I think it may be —— (*Exits off* R., *her laugh is heard, and she returns.*) Yes, it is—our guest of honor! (*Crosses* L., *to down* L. *end of love-seat. Men rise.* JOHN *comes in, immaculately groomed and shining, his white linen coat over his arm. He is a startling contrast to the other male company, who seem to be outcasts of a state in which he is a prominent citizen.*) Everybody, this is Dr. John Buchanan, Jr.

JOHN. (*Crossing to* ALMA L., *easily glancing about the assemblage.*) Hello, everybody.

MRS. BASSETT. I never thought he'd show up. Congratulations, Miss Alma.

JOHN. Did I miss much?

ALMA. Not a thing! Just the minutes—I'll put you on the love-seat. Next to me. (*On hearing this,* ROGER *steps down to look questioningly at* ALMA, *who does not meet his gaze.* JOHN *grins at him, whereupon* ROGER *crosses* R. *to front of chair* R. *of table, and indicates to* VERNON *that he will change seats with him.* VER-

33

NON *backs up stage, gets other high-backed chair from up* R. *and brings it down on a line with other chair, and he and* ROGER *finally seat themselves.* ALMA *has taken* JOHN'S *coat and crosses to fire-rail, putting down coat.*) We mustn't crush this lovely garment. (*She returns to love-seat and sits down, next to* JOHN.) ·Well, now! we are completely assembled!

MRS. BASSETT. (*Eagerly.*) Vernon has his verse play with him to-night!

ALMA. (*Uneasily.*) Is that right, Vernon? (*Obviously, it is. He has a* MS. *four inches thick on his knees. Starts to rise, holding out* MS.)

ROGER. (*Reaches out a restraining hand, stopping* VERNON *midway.*) We decided to put that off till cooler weather. (VERNON *sinks back into his chair.*) Miss Rosemary is supposed to read us a paper tonight on William Blake.

MRS. BASSETT. Those dead poets can keep! (JOHN *laughs.*)

ALMA. (*Excitedly jumps up, comes down to front of table.*) Mrs. Bassett, everybody! This is the way I feel about the verse play. It's too important a thing to read under any but ideal circumstances. Not only atmospheric—on some cool evening with music planned to go with it!—But everyone present so that nobody will miss it! Why don't we ——?

ROGER. Why don't we take a standing vote on the matter?

ALMA. (*Clapping her hands.*) Good, good, perfect! (*Moves back to her seat by* JOHN.)

ROGER. All in favor of putting the verse play off till cooler weather —(*He rises.*) stand up! (*Everybody rises but* ROSEMARY, MRS. BASSETT *and* VERNON. ROSEMARY *starts vaguely to rise, but* MRS. BASSETT *jerks her arm.*)

ROSEMARY. Was this a vote?

ROGER. Now, Mrs. Bassett, no rough tactics, please!

ALMA. Has everybody got fans? John, you haven't got one! (*She crosses to table, takes* ROGER'S *fan, returns and gives it to* JOHN; *they both sit on love-seat.* ROGER *sinks back into his chair.* ROSE-MARY, *the librarian, gets up with her paper.*)

ROSEMARY. (*Reading.*) "The Poet—William Blake."

MRS. BASSETT. Insane, insane, that man was a mad fanatic!

ROGER. Now, Mrs. Bassett!

MRS. BASSETT. This is a free country. I can speak my opinion.

34

And I have read *up* on him. Go on, Rosemary. I wasn't criticizing your paper. (ROSEMARY *is hurt.*)

ALMA. Mrs. Bassett is only joking, Rosemary.

ROSEMARY. No, I don't want to read it if she feels that strongly about it. (*Sits back down,* L. *end piano bench.*)

MRS. BASSETT. Not a bit, don't be silly! (*Rises, moves down in back of table.*) I just don't see why we should encourage the writings of people like that who have already gone into a drunkard's grave!

JOHN. He did?

ROGER. I never heard that about him.

ALMA. (*Rising.*) Mrs. Bassett is mistaken about that. Mrs. Bassett, you have confused Blake with someone else.

MRS. BASSETT. (*Positively.*) Oh, no, don't tell me. I've read up on him and know what I'm talking about. He travelled around with that Frenchman who took a shot at him and landed them both in jail! Brussels, Brussels!

ROGER. (*Turning away.*) Brussels sprouts!

MRS. BASSETT. That's where it happened, fired a gun at him in a drunken stupor, and later one of them died of T. B. in the gutter! (*Pauses, looking around.*) All right. I'm finished. I won't say anything more. (*She reseats herself.*) Go on with your paper, Rosemary. There's nothing like contact with culture!

ALMA. Before Rosemary reads her paper on Blake, I think it would be a good idea, since some of us aren't acquainted with his work, to preface the critical and biographical comments with a reading of one of his loveliest lyric poems.

ROSEMARY. I'm not going to read anything at all! Not I!

ALMA. Then let me read it, then. . . . (*She crosses and takes paper from* ROSEMARY, *then moves down* C. *below table, her back to audience. Group assume various attitudes of listening.*) This is called "Love's Secret." (*She reads.*)

> Never seek to tell thy love,
> Love that never told can be,
> For the gentle wind doth move
> Silently, invisibly.
> I told my love, I told my love,
> I told him all my heart.
> Trembling, cold in ghastly fear
> Did my love depart.

No sooner had he gone from me
Than a stranger passing by,
Silently, invisibly,
Took him with a sigh!

(*Applause.* ALMA *moves up and returns the paper to* ROSEMARY.)

MRS. BASSETT. Honey, you're right. That isn't the man I meant. (*She rises, moves to table, looking at* ROGER.) I was thinking about the one who wrote about " the bought red lips." (*Crosses L. and sits by* JOHN *on love-seat.*) Who was it that wrote about the " bought red lips "? (JOHN *rises abruptly, starts* R. *to door.*)

ALMA. John!

JOHN. (*Calling back as he goes off* R.) I have to call on a patient!

ALMA. Oh, John! (*She rushes down, picks up his coat off fire-rail, goes out after him. A moment of silence as group follow her exit. Then* ROSEMARY *rises, interpreting this as a cue to read her paper.*)

ROSEMARY. "The poet William Blake was born in 1757 ——"

ROGER. Of poor but honest parents.

MRS. BASSETT. No supercilious comments out of you, sir! Go on, Rosemary. She has such a beautiful *voice!* (ALMA *returns, looking stunned. Crosses to* ROSEMARY, *up* C. L., *between her and* MRS. BASSETT.)

ALMA. Please excuse the interruption, Rosemary. Dr. Buchanan had to call on a patient.

MRS. BASSETT. (*Archly.*) I bet I know who the patient was! Ha-ha! That Gonzales girl whose father owns Moon Lake Casino and goes everywhere with a pistol strapped on his belt. Johnny Buchanan will get himself shot in that crowd!

ALMA. Why, Mrs. Bassett, what gave you such an idea? I don't think that John even knows that Gonzales girl!

MRS. BASSETT. He knows her, all right. In the Biblical sense of the word, if you'll excuse me!

ALMA. (*Moves down* C. L., *facing out.*) No, I will not excuse you! A thing like that is inexcusable!

MRS. BASSETT. Have you fallen for him, Miss Alma? Miss Alma has fallen for the young doctor! They tell me he has lots of new lady patients!

ALMA. (*Swings suddenly around, pounds on table with her fists.*) Stop it! I won't have malicious talk here! (*Crosses up* L. *to* MRS. BASSETT.) You drove him away from the meeting after I'd bragged so much about how bright and interesting you all were! You put your worst foot forward and simpered and chattered and carried on like idiots, idiots! What am I saying? I—I—please excuse me! (*Rushes off* R.)

ROGER. (*Rising.*) I move that the meeting adjourn. (VERNON *rises, puts his chair back in place, up* R., *starts out* R.)

MRS. BASSETT. (*Going out* R.) I second the motion. Poor Miss Alma!

ROGER. (*Following her off, carrying minute-book with him.*) She hasn't been herself lately . . .

ROSEMARY. (*Slowly, wonderingly, as she makes her way off* R.) I don't understand. What happened? (*Lights dim out to complete black in rectory. Lighting on angel and on sky dims up.*)

## END OF SCENE

(NOTE: As the people concerned in the foregoing scene exit, they must take their props, fans, etc., with them.)

## PART I

### SCENE 5

*Interior of* DOCTOR'S *office.*
*Lights come on in office and on cyclorama.*
JOHN, *seated in chair in front of desk, has a wound on his arm, which he is trying to bandage.* ROSA *is seated on the couch, with a half-full glass of whiskey in her hand.*

JOHN. (*Holding out his arm, one hand holding end of bandage.*) Hold that end. (ROSA *rises, crosses to him, puts glass on desk, sits on down-stage end of desk, takes hold of bandage.*) Wrap it around. Pull it tight. (*She does so.* ALMA *has entered on ramp from* R., *crosses* L. *to steps, and descends to door of office. She knocks.* JOHN *and* ROSA *look up silently.* ALMA *knocks again.*) I better answer that before they wake up the old man. (*Rolling down his sleeve to conceal bandage, he rises, crosses to door up* R., *opens it.* ALMA *comes in, but stops short at sight of* ROSA. *Lights build up.*) Wait outside, Rosa. In the hall. But be quiet!

37

(ROSA *gives* ALMA *a challenging look as she withdraws off* L., *taking whiskey glass with her.*) A little emergency case. (JOHN *crosses* L. *below desk to* L. *of it.*)

ALMA. The patient you had to call on. (JOHN *grins.*) I want to see your father.

JOHN. (*Moving* R. *a step.*) He's asleep. Anything I can do?

ALMA. No, I think not. I have to see your father.

JOHN. It's two A. M., Miss Alma.

ALMA. I know, I'm afraid I'll have to see him.

JOHN. What's the trouble? (*Voice of* DOCTOR, *calling from above.*)

DR. BUCHANAN, SR.'S VOICE. (*Off* L.) John! What's going on down there?

JOHN. (*Crossing to down* L.) Nothing much, Dad. Somebody got cut in a fight.

VOICE. I'm coming down.

JOHN. No. Don't! Stay in bed! (*Rolls up sleeve to show* ALMA *bandaged wound. She gasps, sinks on couch* R.) I've patched him up, Dad. You sleep!

ALMA. You've been in a brawl with that—woman!

JOHN. (*Nods, rolls sleeve back down. Crossing to up* L. *end of desk.*) Is your *doppelganger* cutting up again?

ALMA. It's your father I want to talk to.

JOHN. Be reasonable, Miss Alma. You're not that sick.

ALMA. (*Rises, crosses to desk, leans on it, facing him.*) Do you suppose I would come here at two o'clock in the morning if I were not seriously ill?

JOHN. (*Crossing to small table* L.) It's no telling what you would do in a state of hysteria. (*Puts some tablets in a glass, pours water from thermos jug into it, crosses to her above desk to her* R.) Toss that down, Miss Alma.

ALMA. What is it?

JOHN. A couple of little white tablets dissolved in water.

ALMA. What kind of tablets?

JOHN. (*Grinning.*) You don't trust me?

ALMA. (*Crosses* L., *sits in chair front of desk.*) You are not in any condition to inspire much confidence. (*She is facing front, seemingly about to lose control and burst into tears.* JOHN, *sensing this, crosses to her, puts glass on desk, puts his hands gently on her shoulders.*) I seem to be all to pieces.

JOHN. The intellectual meeting wore you out.

38

ALMA. You made a quick escape from it.

JOHN. (*Sitting on front edge of desk.*) I don't like meetings. The only meetings I like are between two people.

ALMA. Such as between yourself and the lady outside?

JOHN. Or between you and me.

ALMA. (*Turns to him, nervously.*) Where is the —— (*Reaching for glass of medicine.*)

JOHN. Oh. You've decided to take it? (*Hands her glass. She sips and chokes.*) Bitter?

ALMA. Awfully bitter.

JOHN. (*Taking glass from her, puts it on desk.*) It'll make you sleepy.

ALMA. I do hope so. I wasn't able to sleep.

JOHN. And you felt panicky?

ALMA. Yes. I felt walled in.

JOHN. You started hearing your heart?

ALMA. Yes, like a drum!

JOHN. (*Takng watch from vest pocket.*) It scared you?

ALMA. It always does.

JOHN. Sure. I know.

ALMA. I don't think I will be able to get through the summer.

JOHN. You'll get through it, Miss Alma.

ALMA. How?

JOHN. One day will come after another and one night will come after another till sooner or later the summer will be all through with, and then it will be fall, and you will be saying, I don't see how I'm going to get through the fall.

ALMA. —Oh . . .

JOHN. That's right. Draw a deep breath!

ALMA. —Ah . . .

JOHN. Good. Now draw another!

ALMA. —Ah . . .

JOHN. Better?

ALMA. A little.

JOHN. Soon you'll be much better. (*With watch in one hand, he reaches for her wrist. Holding up watch.*) Did y' know that time is one side of the four-dimensional continuum we're caught in?

ALMA. What?

JOHN. Did you know space is curved, that it turns back onto itself like a soap-bubble, adrift in something that's even less than space?

ROSA. (*Faintly, outside.*) Johnny! (ALMA *turns toward voice.*)

JOHN. Did you know that the Magellanic clouds are a hundred thousand light years away from the earth? No? (ALMA *shakes head slightly.*) That's something to think about when you worry over your heart, that little red fist that's got to keep knocking, knocking against the big black door. (*Drops her wrist.*)

ROSA. (*More distinctly.*) Johnny!

JOHN. Cállate la boca! (*To* ALMA.) There's nothing wrong with your heart but a little functional disturbance, like I told you before. You want me to check it? (ALMA *nods mutely.* JOHN *rises, crosses to above desk, puts watch on desk, opens top* L. *drawer, takes out stethoscope.*)

ALMA. (*Rises, crosses to* R. C.) The lady outside, I hate to keep her waiting.

JOHN. (*Crossing down* L.) Rosa doesn't mind waiting. Unbutton your blouse. (*Hangs stethoscope around his neck.*)

ALMA. Unbutton ——?

JOHN. The blouse. (*Turns chair so it faces down-stage.*)

ALMA. Hadn't I better—better come back in the morning, when your father will be—able to ——?

JOHN. Just as you please, Miss Alma. (ALMA *crosses to chair and sits, her fingers fumbling with buttons on her blouse.*) Fingers won't work?

ALMA. (*Breathlessly.*) They are just as if frozen!

JOHN. (*Kneels by her* L. *side.*) Let me. (*Leans over her, unbuttoning her blouse.*) Little pearl buttons . . .

ALMA. —If your father discovered that woman in the house ——

JOHN. He won't discover it.

ALMA. It would distress him terribly.

JOHN. Are you going to tell him?

ALMA. Certainly not!

JOHN. (*Laughs, applies stethoscope to her chest.*) Breathe!—Out! (*She follows his directions.*) Breathe!—Out!

ALMA. —Ah . . .

JOHN. —Um-hmmmm . . . (*Rises, crosses up above desk, putting stethoscope down.*)

ALMA. What do you hear?

JOHN. (Crossing R., R. end of desk.) —Just a little voice saying—
" Miss Alma is lonesome! "

ALMA. (Rising, crossing up toward door up R.) If your idea of
helping a patient is to ridicule and insult ——

JOHN. (Grabs her by shoulders and stops her.) My idea of helping you is to tell you the truth. (ALMA's hand has been lifted to
ward him off. He takes hold of it and looks at ring on her finger.)
What is this stone?

ALMA. A topaz.

JOHN. Beautiful stone.—Fingers still frozen?

ALMA. A little. (He lifts her hand to his mouth and blows his
breath on her fingers.)

JOHN. (Leads her gently to couch, seats her.) I'm a poor excuse
for a doctor, I'm much too selfish. (Leaning against R. side of
desk.) But let's try to think about you.

ALMA. Why should you bother about me?

JOHN. You know I like you and I think you're worth a lot of
consideration.

ALMA. Why?

JOHN. Because you have a lot of feeling in your heart, and that's
a rare thing. It makes you too easily hurt. Did I hurt you tonight?

ALMA. You hurt me when you sprang up from the sofa and rushed
from the rectory in such—in such mad haste that you left your
coat behind you!

JOHN. I'll pick up the coat some time.

ALMA. The time of our last conversation you said you would take
me riding in your automobile some time, but you forgot to.

JOHN. I didn't forget. Many's the time I've looked across at the
rectory and wondered if it would be worth trying, you and
me . . .

ALMA. You decided it wasn't?

JOHN. I went there tonight, but it wasn't you and me.—Fingers
warm now?

ALMA. Those tablets work quickly. I'm already feeling drowsy.
(Leans back, her eyes nearly shut.) I'm beginning to feel almost
like a water lily. A water lily on a Chinese lagoon. (A heavy
iron bell strikes three off L.)

ROSA. Johnny?

ALMA. (Rises, crosses up to door.) I must go.

JOHN. (Crosses to table L., front of folding screen, gets box of

41

*tablets.*) I will call for you Saturday night at eight o'clock.

ALMA. (*Crossing down two steps.*) What?

JOHN. (*Crossing R., below desk to her, with tablets.*) I'll give you this box of tablets, but watch how you take them. Never more than one or two at a time.

ALMA. Didn't you say something else a moment ago?

JOHN. I said I would call for you at the rectory Saturday night.

ALMA. Oh . . .

JOHN. Is that all right? (ALMA *nods speechlessly. She remains with box resting in palm of her hand as if not knowing it was there.* JOHN *gently closes her fingers on box.*)

ALMA. Oh! (*Laughs faintly.*)

ROSA. (*Enters from L., crosses up to up L. end of desk.*) Johnny! (ALMA *goes out hastily and exits R. Lights in office dim and glow comes on chart of anatomy.*)

JOHN. Do you think you can find your way home, Miss Alma? (*As* JOHN *closes door,* ROSA *crosses to front of chart.* JOHN *crosses to her, takes her roughly in his arms, kisses her. Lights in office dim to complete black. Then lights dim up on the figure of the angel.*)


## END OF SCENE


## PART I

### SCENE 6

*Lights in rectory dim up. Lights on sky cyclorama also come up, with stars visible.*

MR. *and* MRS. WINEMILLER *are discovered in rectory. He is seated in chair R. of table, writing his sermon.* MRS. WINEMILLER *sits on love-seat, indolently fanning herself.* ALMA *runs in from R., crosses up, puts hat and gloves on piano bench up C.*

ALMA. What time is it, Father? (*He goes on writing. She crosses down to table.*) What time is it, Father?

WINEMILLER. (*Takes out watch.*) Five of eight. I'm working on my sermon. (*Puts watch back in pocket.*)

ALMA. Why don't you work in the study?

WINEMILLER. The study is suffocating. So don't disturb me.

ALMA. (*Glances at* MRS. WINEMILLER; *then to* WINEMILLER.) Would there be any chance of getting Mother upstairs if someone should call?

WINEMILLER. Are you expecting a caller?

ALMA. Not expecting. There is just a chance of it.

WINEMILLER. Whom are you expecting?

ALMA. (*Moving* L. *two steps.*) I said I wasn't expecting anyone, that there was just a possibility ——

WINEMILLER. Mr. Doremus? I thought that this was his evening with his mother?

ALMA. Yes, it is his evening with his mother.

WINEMILLER. Then who is coming here, Alma?

ALMA. Probably no one. Probably no one at all. (*Crosses up, sits piano bench.*)

WINEMILLER. This is all very mysterious.

MRS. WINEMILLER. That boy next door is coming to see her, that's who's coming to see her. (*Pulls her dress up over her knees.*)

ALMA. (*Rises, crosses to* MRS. WINEMILLER, *kneels, pulls down dress.*) If you will go upstairs, Mother, I'll call the drugstore and ask them to deliver a pint of fresh peach ice-cream.

MRS. WINEMILLER. I'll go upstairs when I'm ready—good and ready, and you can put that in your pipe and smoke it—Miss Winemiller! (*Pulls up her dress again.*)

ALMA. (*Rises, crosses to above table* C.) I may as well tell you who might call, so that if he calls there will not be any unpleasantness about it. Young Dr. Buchanan said he might call.

MRS. WINEMILLER. (*Jumps up, crosses to between sofa and piano-bench.*) See!

WINEMILLER. (*Taking off his glasses.*) You can't be serious.

ALMA. (*Crossing* L. *to window.*) Well, I am.

MRS. WINEMILLER. Didn't I tell you?

WINEMILLER. (*Rises.*) That young man might come here?

ALMA. He asked me if he might and I said yes, if he wished to. But it is now after eight, so it doesn't look like he's coming.

WINEMILLER. If he does come you will go upstairs to your room and I will receive him. (MRS. WINEMILLER *crosses down to above table.*)

ALMA. If he does come I'll do no such thing, Father. (*Crosses up to love-seat, sits.*)

WINEMILLER. (*Crosses up* L. *to* ALMA.) You must be out of your mind.

ALMA. I'll receive him myself. You may retire to your study, and Mother upstairs. (MRS. WINEMILLER *crosses down, sits in chair* R. *of table.*) But if he comes I'll receive him. I don't judge people by the tongues of gossips. I happen to know that he has been grossly misjudged and misrepresented by old busybodies who're envious of his youth and brilliance and charm!

WINEMILLER. If you're not out of your senses, then I'm out of mine. (MRS. WINEMILLER *furtively lights cigarette.*)

ALMA. I daresay we're all a bit peculiar, Father. . . .

WINEMILLER. Well, I have had one almost insufferable cross to bear—(*Crosses to* MRS. WINEMILLER, *takes cigarette out of her mouth, puts it out.*) and perhaps I can bear another. But if you think I'm retiring into my study when this young man comes, probably with a whiskey bottle in one hand and a pair of dice in the other—(ALMA *rises, steps down* L.) you have another think coming. (*He crosses to table, picks up his sermon, crosses to front of love-seat.*) I'll sit right here and look at him until he leaves. (*Sits on love-seat. A whistle is heard outside,* R.)

ALMA. (*Crosses up to piano bench, picks up hat and gloves.*) As a matter of fact I think I'll walk down to the drugstore and call for the ice-cream myself. (*She rushes out* R.)

MRS. WINEMILLER. (*Rises, crosses up above table.*) There she goes to him! Ha-ha!

WINEMILLER. (*Looking up.*) Alma! Alma! (*Rises, crosses to door.*) Where is Alma?—Alma! (*Goes out* R.)

MRS. WINEMILLER. (*Circles* L. *to down-stage, following him out* R.) Ha-ha! Who got fooled? Who got fooled! Ha-haaa! Insufferable cross yourself, you old—windbag . . . (*She exits* R. WINE-MILLER, *off, calls "Alma!" Lights dim out to black, except sky lights and star effect.*)


## END OF SCENE


(NOTE: When ALMA rushes from rectory in this scene, she runs behind cyclorama to stage L. for her next entrance.)

# PART I

## SCENE 7

*A delicately suggested arbor. This tiny set may be placed way downstage in front of the two interiors. In the background, as it is throughout the play, the angel of the fountain is dimly seen.*

*This arbor set is set in the blackout. When it is in place, DUSTY, the waiter, enters from off L., carrying table with lamp fastened to it, crosses DOCTOR'S office in dark. When he has placed table in front of arbor, a spotlight—leaf effect—from front balcony comes on. DUSTY strikes match and lights lamp on table—amber spot on table area. After table area has been lighted, dim up general playing lights. DUSTY goes off L., reenters with two chairs, which he places one on either side of table. JOHN'S voice is audible before he and ALMA enter, from L.*

JOHN. (*Off.*) I don't understand why we can't go in the casino.

ALMA. (*Descends steps L., crosses down L., followed by JOHN.*) You do understand. You're just pretending not to. (*DUSTY exits up steps R. and goes off L.*)

JOHN. Give me one reason.

ALMA. I am a minister's daughter.

JOHN. That's no reason. (*Turns up stage and calls off L.*) Boy!

ALMA. (*Crossing to R. end of table.*) You're a doctor. That's a better reason. You can't any more afford to be seen in such places than I can—less!

JOHN. (*Bellowing.*) Dusty! Hey, Dusty!

DUSTY. (*Off.*) Yes, sir!

JOHN. (*At L. end of table, turns and faces ALMA, who is busy looking for something in her handbag.*) What are you fishing in that pocketbook for?

ALMA. Nothing.

JOHN. (*Crossing to her.*) What have you got there? (*Taking hold of her bag.*)

ALMA. Let go!

JOHN. (*Takes bag from her, sees box of pills in it.*) Those sleeping tablets I gave you?

45

ALMA. Yes.

JOHN. What for?

ALMA. I need one.

JOHN. *Now?*

ALMA. Yes.

JOHN. Why?

ALMA. Why? Because I nearly died of heart failure in your automobile. What possessed you to drive like that? A demon? (*She sits chair* R. *of table.* DUSTY *enters from* L. *Descends steps* L. *to* JOHN.)

JOHN. (*Crosses toward him, throwing bag on table. As he does so,* ALMA *reaches for it, but* JOHN *puts his hand on it, preventing her from getting it. To* DUSTY.) A bottle of vino rosso.

DUSTY. Yes, sir. (*Starts out* L.)

JOHN. Hey! (DUSTY *stops on steps.*) Tell Shorty I want to hear [*Designate title of some old popular music record*]. (DUSTY *goes out* L. JOHN *turns back to* ALMA.)

ALMA. Please give me back my tablets.

JOHN. (*Tosses bag on his side of table.*) You want to turn into a dope-fiend taking this stuff? I said take one when you need one.

ALMA. I need one now.

JOHN. Sit down and stop swallowing air. (DUSTY *returns with tall wine bottle and two thin-stemmed glasses, puts them on table. Music record offstage.*) When does the cock-fight start?

DUSTY. 'Bout ten o'clock, Dr. Johnny. (*Exits off* L.)

ALMA. When does *what* start?

JOHN. They have a cock-fight here every Saturday night. Ever seen one? (*Pours drink for her, puts it in front of her.*)

ALMA. Perhaps in some earlier incarnation of mine. (JOHN *looks at her, then pours drink for himself.*)

JOHN. (*Sits chair* L. *of table.*) You're going to see one tonight.

ALMA. Oh, no, I'm not.

JOHN. That's what we came here for.

ALMA. I didn't think such exhibitions were legal.

JOHN. (*Drinking.*) This is Moon Lake Casino, where anything goes. (*Leans back in his chair.*)

ALMA. And you're a frequent patron?

JOHN. I'd say constant.

ALMA. Then I'm afraid you must be serious about giving up your medical career.

JOHN. (*Rises, pours himself another drink.*) You bet I'm serious about it. A doctor's life is walled in by sickness and misery and death. (*Drinks, puts bottle on table.*)

ALMA. May I be so presumptuous as to inquire what you'll do when you quit?

JOHN. You may be so presumptuous as to inquire.

ALMA. But you won't tell me?

JOHN. (*Sits on table, L. end.*) I haven't made up my mind, but I've been thinking of South America lately.

ALMA. (*Sadly.*) Oh . . .

JOHN. I've heard that cantinas are lots more fun than saloons, and señoritas are caviar among females. (*Music fades out.*)

ALMA. Dorothy Sykes' brother went to South America and was never heard of again. (JOHN *drinks.*) It takes a strong character to survive in the tropics. Otherwise it's a quagmire.

JOHN. (*Leaning toward her.*) You think my character's weak?

ALMA. I think you're confused, just awfully, awfully confused, as confused as I am—but in a different way. . . .

JOHN. (*Rises, crosses down, sprawls out on bench, leaning on elbow, one foot up on bench.*) Hee-haw, ho-hum!

ALMA. You used to say that as a child—to signify your disgust!

JOHN. (*Grinning.*) Did I? (*Drinks.*)

ALMA. (*Sharply.*) Don't sit like that!

JOHN. Why not?

ALMA. You look so indolent and worthless!

JOHN. Maybe I am.

ALMA. If you must go somewhere, why don't you choose a place with a bracing climate?

JOHN. (*Straightens up, looks at her, grinning.*) Parts of South America are as cool as a cucumber.

ALMA. I never knew that.

JOHN. Well, now you do.

ALMA. Those Latins all dream in the sun—and indulge their senses.

JOHN. You know who's crowned with most of the glory on this earth? The one who uses his senses to get all he can in the way of—satisfaction. (*He drinks.*)

ALMA. Self-satisfaction?

JOHN. What other kind is there?

ALMA. I will answer that question by asking you one.—Have you ever seen, or looked at, a picture of a Gothic cathedral?

47

JOHN. Gothic cathedral—what about it?

ALMA. (*Rises, crosses down above bench.*) How everything reaches up, how everything seems to be straining for something out of the reach of stone—or human—fingers?—The immense stained windows, the great arched doors that are five or six times the height of the tallest man—the vaulted ceiling and all the delicate spires—all reaching up to something beyond attainment! To me—well, that is the secret, the principle back of existence—the everlasting struggle and aspiration for more than our human limits have placed in our reach.—Who was it that said that—oh, so beautiful a thing! —" All of us are in the gutter "—(*She looks up, stretching out her hand.*) " but some of us are looking at the stars! "

JOHN. (*Takes her hand and shakes it.*) Mr. Oscar Wilde.

ALMA. (*Somewhat taken aback.*) —Well, regardless of who said it, it's still true. (*Puts her other hand on his.*) Some of us are looking at the stars!

JOHN. It's no fun holding hands with gloves on, Miss Alma.

ALMA. (*Withdrawing her hands.*) That's easily remedied. I'll just take the gloves off. (*Starts to remove her gloves.*)

JOHN. (*Rises abruptly, crosses up L.*) Christ! (*Music is heard from Casino, some popular tune of the day. He lights a cigarette. He listens for a moment, looking off L.*) Rosa Gonzales is dancing.

ALMA. (*Sits chair R. of table.*) You hate me for depriving you of the company inside. Well—you'll escape bye-and-bye. You'll drive me home and come back out by yourself. I've only gone out with three young men at all seriously, and with each one there was a desert between us.

JOHN. What do you mean by a desert?

ALMA. Oh—wide, wide stretches of uninhabitable ground.

JOHN. (*Puts his foot up on chair, L.*) Maybe you made it that way by being stand-offish?

ALMA. I made quite an effort with one or two of them.

JOHN. What kind of an effort?

ALMA. Oh, I—tried to entertain them the first few times. I would play and sing for them in the rectory parlor.

JOHN. With your father in the next room and the door half open?

ALMA. I don't think that was the trouble.

JOHN. What was the trouble?

ALMA. I—I didn't have my heart in it. (*Laughs uncertainly.*) A silence would fall between us. You know, a silence?

JOHN. Yes, I know, a silence.

ALMA. I'd try to talk, and he'd try to talk, and neither would make a go of it.

JOHN. The silence would fall?

ALMA. Yes, the enormous silence.

JOHN. Then you'd go back to the piano?

ALMA. I'd twist my ring. Sometimes I twisted it so hard that the band cut my finger!—He'd glance at his watch and we'd both know that the useless undertaking had come to a close. . . .

JOHN. You'd call it quits? (*Takes foot off chair, puts out cigarette.*)

ALMA. Quits is—what we'd call it. . . . One or two times I was rather sorry about it.

JOHN. But you didn't have your heart in it?

ALMA. None of them really engaged my serious feelings.

JOHN. (*Moves in above table, half sits on it, facing her.*) You do have serious feelings—of that kind?

ALMA. Doesn't everyone—sometimes?

JOHN. Some women are cold. Some women are what is called frigid.

ALMA. Do I give that impression? (*Music offstage stops.*)

JOHN. (*Leans toward her.*) Under the surface you have a lot of excitement, a great deal more than any other woman I have met. So much that you have to carry these sleeping pills with you.— The question is, why? (*Leans over and lifts her veil.*)

ALMA. What are you doing that for?

JOHN. So that I won't get your veil in my mouth when I kiss you.

ALMA. (*Faintly.*) Do you want to do that?

JOHN. (*Gently.*) Miss Alma! (*Takes her arms, draws her to her feet.*) Oh, Miss Alma, Miss Alma! (*Kisses her.*)

ALMA. (*In a low, shaken voice.*) Not "Miss" any more. Just Alma.

JOHN. (*Grinning gently.*) "Miss" suits you better, Miss Alma. (*Kisses her again. She returns his kiss, then hesitantly touches his shoulders, but not quite to push him away. JOHN continues softly.*) Is it so hard to forget you're a preacher's daughter?

ALMA. There is no reason to forget that I am a minister's daughter. A minister's daughter's no different from any other young lady who tries to remember that she *is* a lady.

JOHN. (*Dropping his arms.*) This lady stuff, is that so important?

49

ALMA. (*Crossing down* R., *facing out.*) Not to the sort of girls that you may be used to bringing to Moon Lake Casino. But suppose that some day—suppose that some day you—married. . . . (JOHN *moves* L., *sits chair* L.) The woman that you selected to be your wife, and not only your wife but—the mother of your children! (*Catches her breath at the thought.*) Wouldn't you want that woman to be a lady? Wouldn't you want her to be somebody that you, as her husband, and they as her precious children—could look up to with very deep respect? (JOHN *makes gesture of impatience.*)

JOHN. There's other things between a man and a woman besides respect. Did you know that, Miss Alma?

ALMA. —Yes. . . .

JOHN. (*Rising, crossing down* L.) There's such a thing as intimate relations.

ALMA. Thank you for telling me that. So plainly.

JOHN. (*Moves in close to her.*) It may strike you as unpleasant. But it does have a good deal to do with— (*Makes a mocking bow to her.*) connubial felicity, as you'd call it. There are some women that just give in to a man as a sort of obligation imposed on them by the—cruelty of nature! (*Turns away from her.*) And there you are.

ALMA. There I am?

JOHN. (*Looking at her.*) I'm speaking generally.

ALMA. Oh. (*Hoarse shouts from Casino.*)

JOHN. (*Crossing up* L., *looking off* L.) The cock-fight has started!

ALMA. (*Crossing up* R., *below table.*) Since you have spoken so plainly, I'll speak plainly, too. (JOHN *turns to face her.*) There are some women who turn a possibly beautiful thing into something no better than the coupling of beasts!—but love is what you bring to it.

JOHN. (*Moves to* L. *of table, on a line with her.*) You're right about that.

ALMA. Some people bring just their bodies. But there are some people, there are some women, John—who can bring their hearts to it, also—who can bring their souls to it!

JOHN. (*Derisively.*) Souls again, huh?—those Gothic cathedrals you dream of! (*Another hoarse prolonged shout from Casino.*) Your name is Alma and Alma is Spanish for soul. Some time I'd like to show you a chart of the human anatomy that I have in the office. It shows what our insides are like, and maybe you can show me where the beautiful soul is located on the chart. (*Music from Casino, voices fade.*) Let's go watch the cock-fight. (*Starts up* L.)

ALMA. (*Crossing down* R., R. *end of bench.*) No! (*Pause.*)

JOHN. (*Crossing down* L., L. *end of bench.*) I know something else we could do.—There are rooms above the Casino . . .

ALMA. (*Back stiffens.*) I'd heard that you made suggestions like that to girls that you go out with, but I refused to believe such stories were true.—What made you think I might be amenable to such a suggestion?

JOHN. I counted your pulse in the office the night you ran out because you weren't able to sleep.

ALMA. (*Moving in to him.*) The night I was ill and went to your father for help?

JOHN. It was me you went to.

ALMA. It was your father, and you wouldn't call your father.

JOHN. Fingers frozen stiff when I ——

ALMA. Oh! I want to go home. But I won't go with you. I will go in a taxi! (*She wheels about hysterically, crosses up* R.) Boy! Boy! Call a taxi!

JOHN. I'll call one for you, Miss Alma. (*Turns up* L., *calling off* L.) Taxi!

ALMA. (*Wildly.*) *You're not a gentleman!*

JOHN. (*Crossing up steps* L., *and off* L., *shouting.*) Taxi!

ALMA. (*Following him to* L. C., *looking after him.*) *You're not a gentleman!* (*Music swells, then fades with falling of curtain.*)

### THE CURTAIN FALLS

### END OF PART I

# PART II

## Scene 1

*At rise, night. Lights on cyclorama, star effect. Rectory interior is lighted.*

*ALMA and ROGER are seated on love-seat in rectory. On table C. is a cut-glass pitcher of lemonade with cherries and orange slices in it, like a little aquarium of tropical fish. ROGER is entertaining ALMA with a collection of photographs and postcards, mementos of his mother's trip to the Orient. He is enthusiastic about them, which he describes in phrases his mother must have assimilated from a sedulous study of literature provided by Cook's Tours. ALMA is less enthusiastic about them.*

ROGER. And this is Ceylon, the Pearl of the Orient! (*Handing ALMA a picture.*)

ALMA. (*Takes picture, looks at it.*) And who is this fat young lady?

ROGER. That is Mother in a hunting costume.

ALMA. The hunting costume makes her figure seem bulky. What was your mother hunting?

ROGER. (*Gaily.*) Heaven knows what she was hunting! But she found Papa.

ALMA. Oh, she met your father on this Oriental tour?

ROGER. Yes. . . . He was returning from India with dysentery and they met on the boat.

ALMA. (*Distastefully.*) Oh. . . . (*Returns picture to ROGER, rises, crosses to table, pours glass of lemonade.*)

ROGER. (*Holding out another picture.*) And here she is on top of a ruined temple!

ALMA. How did she get up there?

ROGER. Climbed up, I suppose.

ALMA. (*Crosses to him, hands him glass.*) What an active woman.

ROGER. (*Takes glass.*) Oh, yes, active is no word for it! (*Gives ALMA another picture.*) Here she is on an elephant's back in Burma.

52

ALMA. (*Holds it up, not really seeing it.*) Ah!

ROGER. (*Drinks, then looks at* ALMA.) You're looking at it upside down, Miss Alma!

ALMA. (*Returning picture to him, with a slight smile.*) Deliberately—to tease you. (*Doorbell rings off* R.) Perhaps that's your mother coming to fetch you home?

ROGER. (*Takes out watch.*) It's ten-fifteen. I never leave till ten-thirty. (*Returns watch to pocket, takes another sip of lemonade.* MRS. BASSETT *enters in a rush.*)

ALMA. (*Crossing* R. *above table.*) Why, Mrs. Bassett! (ROGER *rises.*)

MRS. BASSETT. (*Down* R.) I was just wondering who I could turn to when I saw the rectory light and I thought to myself, Grace Bassett, you trot yourself right over there and talk to Mr. Winemiller!

ALMA. Father has retired.

MRS. BASSETT. Oh, what a pity! (*Crosses* L. *to* ROGER.) Hello, Roger!—I saw that fall your mother took this morning. I saw her come skipping out of the Delta Planter's Bank and I thought to myself, now isn't it remarkable, a woman of her age and weight so light on her feet?—Just at that very moment—*down she went!* I swear to goodness I thought she had broken her hip! *Was* she bruised much?

ROGER. Just shaken up, Mrs. Bassett.

MRS. BASSETT. Oh, how lucky! (*Crosses* R. *to* L. *end table.*) Alma —Alma, if it isn't too late for human intervention, your father's the one right person to call up old Dr. Buchanan at the fever clinic at Lyon and let him know!

ALMA. (*Crossing below chair* R.) About—what?

MRS. BASSETT. You must be stone-deaf if you haven't noticed what's been going on next door since the old Doctor left to fight the epidemic. One continual orgy! Well—not five minutes ago a friend of mine who works at the County court house called to inform me that young Dr. John and Rosa Gonzales have taken a license out—(ALMA *sinks into chair* R.)—and are going to be married tomorrow!

ALMA. Are you—quite certain?

MRS. BASSETT. Certain? I'm always certain before I speak!

ALMA. Why would he—do such a thing?

MRS. BASSETT. August madness! They say it has something to do

53

with the falling stars. Of course, it might also have something to do with the fact that he lost two or three thousand dollars at the Casino, which he can't pay, except by giving himself to Gonzales' daughter. (*Moves in to* ALMA, *who is nervously fingering puzzle on table.*) Alma, what are you doing with that picture puzzle?

ALMA. (*With faint hysterical laugh.*) The pieces don't fit!

MRS. BASSETT. (*To* ROGER.) I should've kept my mouth shut.

ALMA. (*Fiercely, hitting puzzle.*) Will both of you please go! (ROGER *exits hastily* R., *glass still in hand.*)

MRS. BASSETT. (*Moving in back of* ALMA.) I knew this was going to upset you. Goodnight, Alma. (*She exits* R. *Flamenco music is heard from* DOCTOR'S *house, stamping and hand-clapping. Lights come up in* DOCTOR'S *office.* JOHN *enters office interior from* L., *a bottle of champagne in one hand, a champagne glass in other. Weaves unsteadily to couch and sits astride of it, letting bottle slump to floor.*)

ALMA. (*Suddenly springs up, crosses to* L. *end of table, picks up phone.*) Long distance. . . . Please get me the fever clinic at Lyon. . . . I want to speak to Dr. Buchanan! (*Lights in rectory dim to complete black. Music swells.* ALMA *exits* R. *in black, carrying tray out with her.*)

ROSA. (*Calling, off* L.) Johnny! (*She comes in. Lights in office build up. She is dressed in a flamenco costume and has been dancing. Crosses and stands before him. Puts his glass down on couch, touches his face with her finger.*) You have blood on your face!

JOHN. (*Reaches up, pulls her down across his lap.*) You bit my ear.

ROSA. Ohhhh . . . (*Exaggerated concern.*)

JOHN. You never make love without scratching or biting or something. Whenever I leave you I have a little blood on me. Why is that?

ROSA. Because I know I can't hold you.

JOHN. I think you're doing a pretty good job of it. Better than anyone else. (*Kisses her, then puts her on her feet.*) Tomorrow we leave here together, and Father or somebody else can tell old Mrs. Arbuckle her eighty-five years are enough and she's got to go now on the wings of carcinoma. Dance, Rosa! (*She performs a slow and joyless dance before him.*) Tomorrow we leave here together. We sail out of Galveston, don't we? (*Picks up bottle, pours drink and drinks.*)

ROSA. (*As she dances.*) You say it but I don't believe it.

JOHN. I have the tickets.

ROSA. (*Still dancing.*) Two pieces of paper that you can tear in two.

JOHN. We'll go all right, and live on fat remittances from your Papa! Ha-ha!

ROSA. Ha-ha-ha!

JOHN. Not long ago the idea would have disgusted me, but not now. Rosa! (*Catches her by wrist, stopping her dance.*) Rosa Gonzales! Did anyone ever slide downhill as fast as I have this summer? Ha-ha! Like a greased pig. (*Lets go of her, she leans against* R. *edge of desk, watching him.*) And yet every evening I put on a clean white suit. I have a dozen. Six in the closet and six in the wash. And there isn't a sign of depravity in my face. And yet all summer I've sat around here like *this*, remembering last night, anticipating the next one! The trouble with me is, I should have been *castrated!* (*Rises abruptly, with bottle and glass, staggers to above desk, puts them down.* ROSA *has thrown herself on couch, weeping.*) Dance, Rosa! Why don't you dance? (*Crosses to her, pulls her up off couch, holding her hands high.*) What's the matter, Rosa? Why don't you go on dancing?

ROSA. (*Pulls away from him, to* R. C.) *I can't dance any more!*

GONZALES. (*Bellowing triumphantly outside,* L.) *The sky is the limit!*

JOHN. (*Sobered, slumps down on couch.*) Why does your father want me for a son-in-law?

ROSA. *I want you—I—I, want you!*

JOHN. Why do you?

ROSA. (*At* R. *end of desk.*) Maybe because—I was born in Piedras Negras, and grew up in a one-room house with a dirt floor, and all of us had to sleep in that one room, five Mexicans and three geese and a little game-cock named Pepe! Ha-ha! (*Laughs hysterically.*) Pepe was a good fighter! That's how Papa began to make money, winning bets on Pepe! Ha-ha! We all slept in the one room. And in the night I would hear the love-making. Papa would grunt like a pig to show his passion. I thought to myself, how dirty it was, love-making, and how dirty it was to be Mexicans and all have to sleep in one room with a dirt floor and not smell good because there was not any bath-tub!

JOHN. What has that got to do with ——?

55

ROSA. (*Kneels in front of him.*) Me wanting you? (*Embraces him convulsively.*) Ah, but *Quien Sabe!—Quien Sabe!*—Something might happen tonight, and I'll wind up with some dark little friend of Papa's!

GONZALES. (*Off* L., *imperiously.*) Rosa! (*He comes staggering in.*) Rosa!

ROSA. (*Rises, crosses to down* L. *end of desk.*) Si, si, Papa, aqui estoy.

GONZALES. (*Moves to her, unsteadily, and fingers the long strand of gold beads she wears.*) The gold bead . . . (*Suddenly focuses on* JOHN.) Johnny—Johnny! (*Staggers to* JOHN, *catches him in a drunken embrace.*) Listen—when my girl Rosa was little she see a string-a gold bead and she want these gold bead so bad that she cry all night for it. (*Moves to* ROSA, *puts arm around her.*) I don' have money to buy a string-a gold bead—so next day I go for a ride up to Eagle Pass and I walk in a dry-good store and I say to the man—Please give me a string-a gold bead. He say—show me the money, and I say, Here is the money! And I reach down to my belt and I take out—not the money—but this! (*Leaning over* JOHN, *takes out revolver from under his coat.*) Now I have the money, but I still have this. (*Laughs.*) She got the gold bead. Anything that she want I get for her with this—(*Pulls out roll of bills from his* R. *coat pocket.*) or this! (*Waves revolver under* JOHN'S *nose.*)

JOHN. (*Rises, pushes* GONZALES *off, crosses up* R.) Keep your stinking breath out of my face, Gonzales!

ROSA. (*Taking hold of her father.*) Dejalo, dejalo, Papa!

GONZALES. (*Being assisted by* ROSA *to couch.*) Le doy la tierra y si la tierra no basta—le doy el cielo! (*Sinks down on couch.*) The sky is the limit! (*Stretches out on couch, apparently oblivious to everything around him.*)

ROSA. (*To* JOHN.) Let him stay there. Come on back to the party. (*Goes out* L. *Flamenco music fades out, and a different music is heard.* JOHN *turns to window facing rectory. Light in rectory interior builds as* ALMA *enters, in a robe. Crosses to window facing* DOCTOR'S *house. They stand facing each other from opposite interiors as music builds. Slowly, as if drawn by music* JOHN *walks out of office. Music swells. Lights in office dim to black.* JOHN *crosses in back of rectory wall.* ALMA *remains motionless at window until he enters. Music softens.*)

56

JOHN. (*As she turns slowly to face him.*) I took the open door for an invitation. (*Crosses up* L.) The Gulf wind is blowing to-night—cools things off a little.—But my head's on fire. (*She says nothing. Pause.*) The silence? (ALMA *turns, sinks onto love-seat.*) Yes, the enormous silence. (*Lights in* DOCTOR'S *office dim up.* JOHN *moves closer to her.*) I will go in a minute, but first I want you to put your hands on my face. . . . (*Crouches at her feet, takes hold of her hands.*) Eternity and Miss Alma have such cool hands! (*Buries his face in her lap. The attitude suggests a stone Pietà. Lights in rectory dim out to black, and those in office interior dim up slightly. Music fades out and flamenco music is heard again.* NOTE: JOHN *and* ALMA *remain on stage. The old* DOCTOR *comes on from* L. *and enters office, cane and hat in hand. Hat he puts on desk. At almost same time,* ROSA *enters from* L. *and they confront each other.*)

ROSA. Johnny! (*Sees* DOCTOR. *She advances up above* L. *end desk. He faces her at opposite side of desk.*) Oh! I thought you were Johnny! But you're Johnny's father. . . . I—I—I'm Rosa Gonzales!

DOCTOR. I know who you are! What's going on in my house?

ROSA. (*Moving in to him.*) John's giving a party because we're leaving tomorrow. (*Defiantly.*) Yes! Together! I hope you like the idea, but if you don't it don't matter, because *we* like the idea and my father likes the idea!

GONZALES. (*Stupidly, sitting up on couch.*) The sky is the limit!

DOCTOR. (*Turns on* GONZALES, *grabbing him by coat.*) Get your— swine out of—my house! (*Strikes* GONZALES *with his cane.*)

GONZALES. (*Roaring with pain.*) Aieeeee! (*Staggers off couch and backs to* C., *revolver in hand.*)

ROSA. (*Breathlessly, backing against chart of anatomy.*) No! No, Papa!

DOCTOR. (*Advancing on* GONZALES, *cane upraised.*) Get your swine out, I said! Get them out of my house! (*Striking again, drives* GONZALES L. *and out door* L.)

ROSA. (*Wildly and despairingly.*) No, no, no, no, no, no! (*She covers her face. A revolver is fired, off stage* L. *Flamenco m··· c stops short. Simultaneously, more ominous music is heard. Everything dims to black but a spot of light on* ROSA, *standing against chart of anatomy with closed eyes and face twisted like that of a tragic mask. Then all to black.* NOTE: *In this blackout,* JOHN *and*

57

ALMA *go off* R. *and cross back of cyclorama to make their next entrance from stage* L. ROSA, *in the black, takes bottle, glass and* DOCTOR'S *hat, exits off* L. *Slowly a spot dims up on stone angel. Then lights of office interior dim up. Music fades.*)

## END OF SCENE

## PART II

### SCENE 2

*Office interior.*
*Stone angel dimly visible above.*
JOHN *enters from* L., *haggard and dishevelled. Makes his way slowly on stage to front of desk, supports himself there a moment, then moves to couch, slumps down on it. Sounds of* WINEMILLER *making a prayer come through inner door.*

WINEMILLER. (*Off* L.)
    Oh, God, to whom all hearts are open
    And from whom no secrets are hid,
    Help this, Thy servant, in his hour of need.
    And if it be Thy will, O Lord, take him unto Thyself,
    Granting him the peace of life everlasting.
(*During prayer*, ALMA *has entered with a coffee tray, crossing below desk to up* R. *and placed tray on desk.*)
JOHN. What is that mumbo-jumbo your father is spouting in there?
ALMA. (*Pouring coffee.*) A prayer.
JOHN. Tell him to quit. We don't want that worn-out magic.
ALMA. You may not want it, but it's not a question of what you want any more. I've made you some coffee. (*Moves down to him with cup of coffee.*)
JOHN. I don't want any.
ALMA. (*Puts cup back on tray. Picking up towel on tray, she crosses to him.*) Lean back and let me wash your face off, John. (*Presses towel to his face.*) It's such a fine face, a fine and sensitive face, a face that has power in it that shouldn't be wasted.
JOHN. Never mind that. (*Pulls roughly away from her.*)

58

ALMA. (*As she crosses to down* R. *end of desk, puts towel back on tray.*) You have to go in to see him.

JOHN. I couldn't. He wouldn't want me.

ALMA. This happened because of his devotion to you.

JOHN. It happened because some meddlesome Mattie called him back here tonight. Who was it did that?

ALMA. I did.

JOHN. (*Rising.*) It *was* you, then!

ALMA. I phoned him at the fever clinic in Lyon as soon as I learned what you were planning to do. I told him to come here and stop it.

JOHN. You brought him here to be shot.

ALMA. You can't put the blame on anything but your weakness.

JOHN. *You* call me weak?

ALMA. Sometimes it takes a tragedy like this to make a weak person strong.

JOHN. You—white-blooded spinster! You so right people, pious pompous mumblers, preachers and preacher's daughter, all muffled up in a lot of worn-out magic! And I was supposed to minister to your neurosis, give you tablets for sleeping and tonics to give you the strength to go on mumbling your worn-out mumbo-jumbo!

ALMA. Call me whatever you want, but don't let your father hear your drunken shouting. (*Starts away from him* L.)

JOHN. (*Seizes her.*) Stay here!—I want you to look at something. (*Drags her up* R., *holding on to her upper arms, facing her toward anatomy chart.*) This chart of anatomy, look!

ALMA. I've seen it before. (*Turns head away.*)

JOHN. You've never dared to look at it.

ALMA. Why should I?

JOHN. You're scared to.

ALMA. (*Struggling.*) You must be out of your senses.

JOHN. (*Holding her fast.*) You talk about weakness, but can't even look at a picture of human insides.

ALMA. They're not important.

JOHN. That's your mistake. You think you're stuffed with rose-leaves? Turn around and look at it, it may do you good! (*Pulls her around.*)

ALMA. How can you behave like this with your father dying and you so ——? (*Struggling.*)

JOHN. Hold still!

59

ALMA. —so much to blame for it!

JOHN. No more than you are!

ALMA. At least for this little while ——

JOHN. Look here!

ALMA. —You could feel some shame!

JOHN. (*With crazy grinning intensity, holding her fast.*) Now listen here to the anatomy lecture! (*Holding her with one hand, uses R. hand to point to places on chart that he mentions.*) This upper story's the brain, which is hungry for something called truth and doesn't get much but keeps on feeling hungry! This middle's the belly which is hungry for food. This part down here is the sex which is hungry for love because it is sometimes lonesome. (*Releases her arm.*) I've fed all three, as much of all three as I could, or as much as I wanted.—You've fed none—nothing. Well—maybe your belly a little—watery subsistence—but love or truth, nothing but—nothing but hand-me-down notions!—attitudes —poses! Now you can go. (*Crosses down L., front of chair.*) The anatomy lecture is over. (*Sits chair front of desk.*)

ALMA. So that is your high conception of human desires! (*Crosses L. above desk to up L. end of it, indicating chart.*) What you have here is not the anatomy of a beast, but a man. And I reject your opinion of where love is, and the kind of truth you believe the brain to be seeking! (*Crosses down to above him.*) There is something not shown on the chart.

JOHN. You mean the part that Alma is Spanish for, do you?

ALMA. Yes, that's not shown on the anatomy chart! But it's there, just the same, yes, there! Somewhere not seen, but there. And it's *that* that I loved you with—that! Not what you mention. (*Rises and crosses R. to couch.*) Yes, did love you with, John, did nearly *die* of when you hurt me!

JOHN. (*Turned away from her.*) I wouldn't have made love to you.

ALMA. (*Uncomprehendingly, crossing R. between desk and chair to C.*) What?

JOHN. (*Turns to her.*) The night at the Casino—I wouldn't have made love to you. Even if you had consented to go upstairs. I couldn't have made love to you. (*She stares at him as if anticipating some unbearable hurt.*) Yes, yes! Isn't that funny? I'm more afraid of your soul than you're afraid of my body. You'd have been as safe as the angel of the fountain—because I wouldn't feel

60

*decent* enough—to touch you. . . . (*Sinks down on couch.*)
WINEMILLER. (*Entering, from* L., *to down* L.) He's resting more easily now. (JOHN *reaches for coffee cup.*)
ALMA. (*Intercepting him, picks up tray.*) It's cold.
JOHN. It's all right.
ALMA. I'll heat it.
WINEMILLER. (*Moving in.*) Alma, Dr. John wants you.
ALMA. I ——
WINEMILLER. He asked if you would sing for him.
ALMA. I—couldn't—now.
JOHN. Go in and sing to him, Miss Alma! (ALMA *looks at him a moment, then turns and goes off* L., *followed by* WINEMILLER. *After a few moments her voice rises softly within, singing. Lights in interior and on stone angel dim.* JOHN *rises, moves* L. *and clutches desk for support. Takes a step down-stage, then stops. Lights dim. He stands for a moment, gathering courage, then stumblingly starts off* L. *Softly and with deep tenderness.*) Father? (*Lights dim to complete black as he exits. Singing fades. A glow of light appears, lighting angel. Then slowly, cyclorama lighting, for exterior, dims up.*)

## END OF SCENE

## PART II

### SCENE 3

*Cyclorama is a faint blue with late afternoon in autumn. Lights in rectory interior dim up.*
*When it is light,* ALMA *enters rectory interior in a dressing-gown, her hair hanging loose. She looks as if she had been through a long illness, the intensity drained, her pale face listless. She crosses and looks out window. Sits down weakly on sofa and closes her eyes with exhaustion.* MR. *and* MRS. WINEMILLER *enter outer door-frame of rectory, a grotesque-looking couple.* MRS. WINEMILLER *has on her plumed hat, at a rakish angle, and a brilliant scarf about her throat, her face wears a roguish smile that suggests a musical comedy pirate. One hand holds*

WINEMILLER'S *arm and with the other she is holding an ice-cream cone.*

WINEMILLER. (*As they reach* C. *stage.*) Now you may let go of my arm, if you please! (*Takes her hand off his arm roughly.* MRS. WINEMILLER *laughs, moves to chair* R. *of table and sits, licking her cone. He crosses to up* L., *taking off his hat.*) She was on her worst behavior. Stopped in front of the White Star Pharmacy on Front Street and stood there like a mule, wouldn't budge till I bought her an ice-cream cone. I had it wrapped in tissue paper because she had promised me that she wouldn't eat it until we got home. The moment I gave it to her she tore off the paper and walked home licking it every step of the way! (*Crosses toward* MRS. WINEMILLER *angrily, above table.*) . . . just . . . just to humiliate me!

MRS. WINEMILLER. (*Laughs gaily, offers cone to him.*) Lick?

WINEMILLER. (*Angrily.*) No, thank you! (*Puts hat down on piano bench.*)

ALMA. Now, now, children.

WINEMILLER. (*His irritation shifting to* ALMA, *moves* L. *toward her.*) Alma! Why don't you get dressed? It hurts me to see you sitting around like this, day in, day out, like an invalid, when there is nothing particularly wrong with you. I can't read your mind. You may have had some kind of disappointment, but you must not make it an excuse for acting as if the world had come to an end.

ALMA. I have made the beds and washed the breakfast dishes and phoned the market and sent the laundry out and peeled the potatoes and shelled the peas and set the table for lunch. What more do you want? (*Rises, moves to look out window.*)

WINEMILLER. (*Sharply.*) I want you to either get dressed or stay in your room. (*Suddenly.*) At night you get dressed. Don't you? Yes, I heard you slipping out of the house at two in the morning. And that was not the first time.

ALMA. I don't sleep well. Sometimes I have to get up and walk for a while before I am able to sleep.

WINEMILLER. What am I going to tell people who ask about you?

ALMA. (*Crosses* R. *to him.*) Tell them I've changed, and you're waiting to see in what way.

WINEMILLER. Are you going to stay like this indefinitely?

ALMA. Not indefinitely, but you may wish that I had. (*Turns facing out, twisting ring on her finger.*)

WINEMILLER. Stop twisting that ring! Whenever I look at you you're twisting that ring. Give me that ring! I'm going to take that ring off your finger! (*Catches her wrist, they struggle. She breaks roughly away from him to R. C., above table. Faint. band music heard off L.*)

MRS. WINEMILLER. (*Joyfully.*) Fight! Fight!

WINEMILLER. Oh, I give up! (*Sinks into love-seat.*)

ALMA. That's better. (*She hears band music, looks L.*) Is there a parade in town?

MRS. WINEMILLER. Ha-ha—yes! They met him at the station with a big silver loving cup!

ALMA. —Who? Who did they ——?

MRS. WINEMILLER. That boy next door, the one you watched all the time!

ALMA. Is that true, Father?

WINEMILLER. (*Unfolding newspaper.*) Haven't you looked at the papers?

ALMA. No, not lately.

WINEMILLER. (*Wiping his eyeglasses.*) These people are grasshoppers, just as likely to jump one way as another. He's finished the work his father started—stamped out the fever—and gotten all of the glory. (*Rises, moves down to window, looking out.*) Well, that's how it is in this world. Years of devotion and sacrifice are overlooked while someone young and lucky walks off with the honors! (*Band music swells.*)

ALMA. (*Suddenly crying out.*) There he is! (*Staggers back, falls in a heap on piano bench. WINEMILLER turns from window to her, MRS. WINEMILLER rises, moves up above chair. ALMA, faintly.*) What . . . happened? Something . . . struck me!

WINEMILLER. Alma . . . I'll call a doctor.

ALMA. No, no, don't. Don't call anybody to help me. I want to die! (*Lights dim up in office interior: JOHN enters with loving-cup. He is sprucely dressed and his whole manner suggests a new-found responsibility. In rectory, WINEMILLER moves to ALMA, helps her up and leads her off R., followed by MRS. WINEMILLER. As they pass C. stage, lights in rectory dim to black. JOHN looks for a place to put cup, finally crosses L. to table L., puts it down. Then kneels to examine books on lower shelf of table, his back*) *to door.* NELLIE EWELL *appears in up* R. *door behind him. Stands for a moment, then swings door against wall and giggles. She has abruptly grown up, and wears very adult clothes, but has lost none of her childish impudence and brightness.* JOHN *gives a startled whistle as he turns and sees her.*)

JOHN. High heels, feathers . . . and paint!

NELLIE. Not paint!

JOHN. Natural color?

NELLIE. Excitement.

JOHN. Over what?

NELLIE. Everything! You! You here! (JOHN *crosses to above desk.*) Didn't you see me at the depot? I shouted and waved my arm off! I'm home for Thanksgiving.

JOHN. From where?

NELLIE. (*Crossing down below table to down* C.) Sophie Newcomb's. (*She faces him across desk, draws book from under her arm.*) Here is that nasty book you gave me last summer when I was pretending such ignorance of things! (*Tosses book on desk.*)

JOHN. (*Moving down a step.*) Only pretending?

NELLIE. Yes. (*She giggles.*) Well? Shall I go now, or will you look at my tongue? (*Leans over desk from down* R. *end, sticking out her tongue.*)

JOHN. (*Leaning over desk from up* R. *end.*) Red as a berry!

NELLIE. Peppermint drops! Will you have one? (*Holds out sack.*)

JOHN. Thanks. (NELLIE *giggles as he takes one.*) What's the joke, Nellie?

NELLIE. They make your mouth so sweet!

JOHN. So?

NELLIE. I always take one when I hope to be kissed.

JOHN. Suppose I took you up on that?

NELLIE. I'm not scared. Are you? (JOHN *crosses down to down* R. *end desk, leans over and kisses her. She puts her hand on back of his head, pulling him to her, returning his kiss with fervor. He pulls away finally.*)

JOHN. (*Considerably impressed.*) Where did you learn such tricks?

NELLIE. I've been away to school. But they didn't teach me to love.

JOHN. Who are you to be using that long word?

NELLIE. That isn't a long word!

JOHN. (*Moving down a step.*) No? (*She moves eagerly toward him, he takes her by the arms and backs up* R. *with her, toward door.*) Run along, Nellie, before we get into trouble.

NELLIE. Who's afraid of trouble, you or me?

JOHN. I am. Run along! Hear me?

NELLIE. Oh, I'll go now. But I'll be back for Christmas! (*Laughs and runs out. As* JOHN *moves up and closes door behind her, he turns, takes out handkerchief, mops his forehead. Lights black out in office.*)

## END OF SCENE

## PART II

### SCENE 4

*An afternoon in December. Fountain in park. Lights dim up on playing area,* C. *stage, and on cyclorama, clouds appear on the sky. Very windy. (Sound of wind effects offstage.)*

ALMA *enters fountain area from* R. *She seems to move with an effort against the wind. Crosses down steps* R. *and down stage* C., *where she sinks on bench.* MRS. BASSETT, *with a flowing black veil, comes on from* L., *sees* ALMA, *crosses down steps* L., *starts* R.

MRS. BASSETT. Hello, Alma.

ALMA. Good afternoon, Mrs. Bassett.

MRS. BASSETT. Such wind, such wind! (*Wind effect, then dies down.*)

ALMA. Yes, it nearly swept me off my feet. I had to sit down to catch my breath for a moment.

MRS. BASSETT. I wouldn't sit too long if I were you.

ALMA. No, not long.

MRS. BASSETT. (*Crossing down to* R. *end of bench.*) It's good to see you out again after your illness.

ALMA. Thank you.

MRS. BASSETT. Our poor little group broke up after you dropped out.

ALMA. (*Insincerely.*) What a pity!

MRS. BASSETT. You should have come to the last meeting.

ALMA. Why, what happened?

MRS. BASSETT. Vernon read his verse play!

ALMA. And how was it received?

MRS. BASSETT. Maliciously, spitefully and vindictively torn to pieces, the way children tear the wings off butterflies. But I think next spring we might reorganize —— (NELLIE EWELL *enters from* L., *dressed very fashionably and bearing a fancy basket of Christmas packages.*)

NELLIE. (*From top of steps* L.) Hello, Miss Alma! (ALMA *turns up to look at her.*)

MRS. BASSETT. (*Snubbing* NELLIE.) Good-bye, Alma! (*Goes up steps* R. *and off* R.)

NELLIE. (*Coming down steps* L. *to down* L. *end of bench.*) Here you are!

ALMA. Why, Nellie . . . Nellie Ewell!

NELLIE. I was by the rectory. Just popped in for a second; the holidays are so short that every minute is precious. They told me you'd gone to the park.

ALMA. This is the first walk I've taken in quite a while.

NELLIE. You've been ill!

ALMA. Not exactly ill, just not very well. How you've grown up, Nellie!

NELLIE. (*Crossing* R. *below bench to* R., *turns to* ALMA.) It's just my clothes. Since I went off to Sophie Newcomb I've picked out my own clothes, Alma. (*Puts basket down on* R. *end bench.*) When Mother had jurisdiction over my wardrobe, she tried to keep me looking like a child!

ALMA. Your voice is grown-up, too.

NELLIE. They're teaching me diction, Miss Alma. I'm learning to talk like you, long A's and everything such as "cahn't!" and "bahth" and "lahf" instead of "laugh." Yesterday I slipped. I said I "lahfed and lahfed till I nearly died laughing!" (*Giggles, puts basket on ground, sits on bench* R. *end.*) Johnny was so amused at me!

ALMA. Johnny?

NELLIE. Your next-door neighbor!

ALMA. Oh! I'm sure it must be a very fashionable school.

NELLIE. Oh, yes, they're preparing us to be young ladies in so-

ciety. What a pity there's no society here to be a young lady in
. . . at least not for me, with Mother's reputation!

ALMA. You'll find other fields to conquer.

NELLIE. What's this I hear about *you*?

ALMA. I have no idea, Nellie.

NELLIE. That you've quit teaching singing and gone into retire-
ment from the world.

ALMA. Naturally, I had to stop teaching while I was ill, and as for
retiring from the world . . . it's more a case of the world retiring
from me.

NELLIE. I know somebody whose feelings you've hurt badly.

ALMA. Why, who could that be, Nellie?

NELLIE. Somebody who regards you as an angel!

ALMA. I can't think who might hold me in such esteem.

NELLIE. Somebody who says that you refused to see him.

ALMA. I saw nobody. For several months. The long summer wore
me out so.

NELLIE. (*Rises from bench, kneels by basket.*) Well, anyhow, I'm
going to give you your present.

ALMA. Nellie, you shouldn't have given me anything.

NELLIE. I'd like to know why not!

ALMA. I didn't expect it.

NELLIE. After the trouble you took with my horrible voice?
(*Rises, moves in, hands ALMA small package.*)

ALMA. (*Accepting it.*) It's very sweet of you, Nellie.

NELLIE. Open it!

ALMA. Now?

NELLIE. Why, sure.

ALMA. It's so prettily wrapped I hate to undo it.

NELLIE. I love to wrap presents, and since it was for you, I did a
specially dainty job of it.

ALMA. (*Starts to unwrap box.*) I'm going to save this ribbon. I'm
going to keep this lovely paper, too, with the silver stars on it.
And the sprig of holly ——

NELLIE. (*Reaching over and taking holly.*) Let me pin it on your
jacket, Alma. (*Crosses above ALMA on bench, pins holly on her
coat lapel.*)

ALMA. Yes, do. I hardly realized that Christmas was coming. . . .
(*Opens box revealing lace handkerchief and a card.*) What an
exquisite handkerchief!

67

NELLIE. (*At down* R. *end of bench.*) I hate to give people handkerchiefs, it's so unimaginative.

ALMA. I love to get them.

NELLIE. It comes from Maison Blanche!

ALMA. Oh, does it really?

NELLIE. Smell it!

ALMA. Sachet? (*Smells handkerchief,* NELLIE *leans over to sniff, too, giggles.*) Roses! Well, I'm just more touched and pleased than I can possibly tell you!

NELLIE. (*Suddenly.*) The card! (*Starts looking through wrappings on* ALMA'S *lap.*)

ALMA. Card?

NELLIE. (*Seeing it on ground in front of bench, she snatches it up and hands it to* ALMA.) You dropped it.

ALMA. Oh, how clumsy of me! Thank you, Nellie. (*Reading.*) " Joyeaux Noel . . . to Alma . . . from Nellie and " . . . (*She looks up slowly.*) " John ? "

NELLIE. (*Sits on bench.*) He helped me wrap presents last night and when we came to yours we started talking about you. Your ears must have burned!

ALMA. (*Rises, with wrappings and card. Facing out.*) You mean you—spoke well of me?

NELLIE. " Well of "! We raved, simply raved! Oh, he told me the influence you'd had on him!

ALMA. Influence?

NELLIE. He told me about the wonderful talks he'd had with you last summer when he was so mixed up and how you inspired him and you more than anyone else was responsible for his pulling himself together, after his father was killed, and he told me about —— (ALMA *crosses up to* R. *side of fountain.*) Where are you going, Miss Alma? (*Rises, crosses up* L. *above bench, facing* ALMA.)

ALMA. To drink at the fountain. (*She bends over and drinks.*)

NELLIE. He told me about how you came in the house that night like an angel of mercy!

ALMA. (*Looking up at stone angel.*) This is the only angel in Glorious Hill. Her body is stone and her blood is mineral water. (*Wind increases—very loud.*)

NELLIE. (*Hugging herself, facing down.*) How penetrating the wind is!

ALMA. (*On bottom step*, R. *of fountain.*) I'm going home, Nellie. You run along and deliver your presents now. . . . (*Starts up steps.*)

NELLIE. (*Moving up.*) But wait till I've told you the wonder-fullest thing I ——

ALMA. (*Continuing out.*) I'm going home now. Good-bye. (*Goes off* R.)

NELLIE. (*Moves up to base of steps* R., *waves.*) Good-bye, Miss Alma. (*Crosses down, picks up basket, goes up steps* L. *and off* L. *Lights on playing area dim out. Wind softens.*)

## END OF SCENE

## PART II

### SCENE 5

*An hour later. Office interior. Office interior playing lights dim up. Wind is still blowing, softly.*

JOHN *enters from* L., *wearing white doctor's jacket, stethoscope suspended from his neck, carrying a tray with new microscope, test-tubes in a rack, medical instruments. Crosses* R. *below desk and up to above desk, puts tray down. A bell starts to toll the hour of five.* JOHN *looks off, picks up watch from desk, checks the time, replaces watch, starts to examine test-tubes. As last chime sounds,* ALMA *enters office from* L. *She wears a green suit and a matching hat with plume. They stand for a moment, looking at each other.*

ALMA. (*Down* L., *below chair front of desk.*) No greetings? No greetings at all?

JOHN. Hello, Miss Alma.

ALMA. (*Facing out.*) Those new glass cases—ah! Such glacial brilliance!

JOHN. (*Coming down,* R. C.) New equipment.

ALMA. Everything new but the chart.

JOHN. The human anatomy's always the same old thing.

ALMA. And such a tiresome one! I've been plagued with sore throats.

JOHN. Everyone has here lately. These Southern homes are all improperly heated. Open grates aren't enough.

ALMA. They burn the front of you while your back is freezing!

JOHN. Then you go into another room and get chilled off.

ALMA. Yes—yes—chilled to the bone.

JOHN. But it never gets quite cold enough to convince the damn fools that a furnace is necessary, so they go on building without them.

ALMA. Such a strange afternoon.

JOHN. Is it? I haven't been out.

ALMA. The Gulf wind is blowing big, white—what do they call them? Cumulus?—clouds over! It seemed determined to take the plume off my hat—(*Removes her hat.*) like that fox terrier we had once named Jacob, snatched the plume off a hat and dashed around and around the back yard with it like a trophy!

JOHN. I remember Jacob. What happened to him?

ALMA. Oh, Jacob. Jacob was such a mischievous thief. We had to send him out to some friends in the country. Yes, he ended his days as—a country squire! The tales of his exploits ——

JOHN. (*Indicating chair below desk,* L.) Sit down, Miss Alma.

ALMA. If I'm disturbing you ——?

JOHN. No. (ALMA *sits in chair, puts hat, gloves and bag on desk. Wind fades out.* JOHN *sits on couch.*) I called the rectory when I heard you were sick. Your father told me you wouldn't see a doctor.

ALMA. I needed a rest, that was—all. . . . You were out of town mostly . . .

JOHN. I was mostly in Lyon, finishing up Dad's work in the fever clinic.

ALMA. Covering yourself with sudden glory!

JOHN. Redeeming myself with good works.

ALMA. It's rather late to tell you how happy I am, and also how proud. I almost feel as your father might have felt—if —— (JOHN *rises, crosses to above desk.*) And—are you—happy now, John?

JOHN. (*Sits desk chair.*) I've settled with life on fairly acceptable terms. Isn't that all a reasonable person can ask for?

ALMA. He can ask for much more than that. He can ask for the coming true of his most improbable dreams.

JOHN. It's best not to ask for too much.

ALMA. I disagree with you. I say, ask for all, but be prepared to get nothing! (*Rises, crosses up to window, looking out.*) No, I haven't been well. I've thought many times—(*Turns to him.*) of something you told me last summer, that I have a doppelganger. I looked that up and I found that it means another person inside me, another self, and I don't know whether to thank you or not for making me conscious of it! (*Turns to window.*) I haven't been well. . . . For a while I thought I was dying, that that was the change that was coming.

JOHN. When did you have that feeling?

ALMA. August. September. (*Crosses down L. to below chair.*) But now the Gulf wind has blown that feeling away like a cloud of smoke, and I know now I'm not dying, that it isn't going to turn out to be that simple . . .

JOHN. (*Rises, crosses down on her R., takes out watch, puts his fingers on her wrist.*) Have you been anxious about your heart again?

ALMA. And now the stethoscope? (JOHN *looks at her, then crosses to couch, replacing watch in jacket pocket. Sits on couch, takes stethoscope from his neck. She crosses up to him, he places stethoscope in position, starts to listen to her heart. She looks down at his bent head. Slowly, involuntarily, her hands lift and descend on the crown of his head. He looks up at her, then takes off stethoscope. She bends down to a kneeling position in front of him and presses her mouth to his. He is passive. Slowly, she rises.*) Why don't you say anything? Has the cat got your tongue?

JOHN. Miss Alma, what can I say?

ALMA. You've gone back to calling me " Miss Alma " again.

JOHN. We never really got past that point with each other.

ALMA. Oh, yes, we did. We were so close that we almost breathed together!

JOHN. (*Embarrassed.*) I didn't know that.

ALMA. No? Well, I did, I knew it. (*Her hand touches his face tenderly.*) You don't have those little razor cuts on your chin that you dusted with gardenia talcum. . . .

JOHN. (*Gently removing her hand.*) I shave more carefully now.

ALMA. So that explains it! (*Pause.*) Is it—impossible now?

JOHN. I don't think I know what you mean.

ALMA. You know what I mean, all right! So be honest with me. One time I said " no " to something. You may remember the time, and all that demented howling from the cock-fight! (*Puts her hands on his face.*) But now I have changed my mind, or the girl who said "no"—she doesn't exist any more, she died last summer—suffocated in smoke from something on fire inside her. No, she doesn't live now, but she left me her ring—you see? (*She clasps ring on her L. hand with her R. hand, showing it to him.*) This one you admired, the topaz ring set in pearls —— And she said to me when she slipped this ring on my finger— "Remember I died empty-handed,—(*Takes his face in her hands again.*) and so make sure that your hands have *something* in them!" I said, "But what about pride?"—She said, "Forget about pride whenever it stands between you and what you must have!" (*She releases him, turns out.*) —And then I said, "But what if he doesn't want me?" I don't know what she said then— I'm not sure whether she said anything, or not—her lips stopped moving—yes, I think she stopped breathing! (*He is turned away from her.*)—No? (*He does not respond. She crosses down R. end of desk.*) Then the answer is "no"!

JOHN. (*Rises, crosses to her.*) I have a respect for the truth, and I have a respect for you—so I'd better speak honestly if you want me to speak. You've won the argument that we had between us.

ALMA. What—argument?

JOHN. The one about the chart.

ALMA. (*She crosses L. to down L. end of desk, circling to face chart up-stage.*) Oh—the chart!

JOHN. (*Crossing up to up R. end of desk, puts stethoscope down.*) It shows that we're not a package of rose leaves, that every interior inch of us is taken up with something ugly and functional, and no room seems to be left for anything else in there.

ALMA. —No . . .

JOHN. (*Above desk, pushes chair in under desk.*) But I've come around to your way of thinking, that something else is in there, an immaterial something—as thin as smoke—which all of those ugly machines combine to produce, and that's their whole reason for being. It can't be seen so it can't be shown on the chart. But it's there, just the same, and knowing it's there—why, then the whole thing—this—this unfathomable experience of ours—takes on a new value, like some—some wildly romantic work in a laboratory! Don't you see?

ALMA. Yes, I see! Now that you no longer want it to be otherwise you're willing to believe that a spiritual bond *can* exist between us two!

JOHN. Can't you believe that I am sincere about it?

ALMA. Maybe you are. (*Crossing up* L., *on a line with him.*) But I don't want to be talked to like some incurably sick patient you have to comfort. (*A harsh and strong note comes into her voice.*) Oh, I suppose I am sick, one of those weak and divided people who slip like shadows among you solid strong ones. But sometimes, out of necessity, we shadowy people take on a strength of our own. I have that now. You needn't try to deceive me.

JOHN. I wasn't.

ALMA. You needn't try to comfort me. (JOHN *crosses down to couch, sits.*) I haven't come here on any but equal terms. (*Crosses* R. *above desk chair to up* L.) You said, let's talk truthfully. Well, let's do! Unsparingly truthfully, even shamelessly, then! (*Crossing down two steps, above him.*) It's no longer a secret that I love you. It never was. I loved you as long ago as the time I asked you to read the stone angel's name with your fingers. Yes, I remember the long afternoons of our childhood, when I had to stay indoors to practice my music—and heard your playmates calling you, " Johnny! Johnny! " How it went through me, just to hear your name called! And how I—rushed to the window to watch you jump the porch-railing! Stood at a distance, half-way down the block, only to keep in sight of your torn red sweater, racing about the vacant lot you played in. Yes, it had begun that early, this affliction of love, and has never let go of me since, but kept on growing. I've lived next door to you all the days of my life, a weak and divided person who stood in adoring awe of your singleness, of your strength. And that is my story! Now I wish *you* would tell *me* —— Why didn't it happen between us? Why did I fail? Why did you come almost close enough—and no closer?

JOHN. (*Rising.*) Whenever we've gotten together, the three or four times that we have ——

ALMA. As few as that?

JOHN. It's only been three or four times that we've—come face to face. And each of those times—we seemed to be trying to find something in each other without knowing what it was that we wanted to find. It wasn't a body hunger—(*Crosses* L. *to chair below desk.*)—although—I acted as if I thought it might be, the

73

night I wasn't a gentleman—at the Casino —— It wasn't the physical you that I really wanted!

ALMA. (*Crosses down, on a line with him.*) I know, you've already ——!

JOHN. (*Takes cigarette from jacket pocket, puts it in his mouth.*) You didn't have that to give me.

ALMA. Not at that time.

JOHN. You had something else to give. (*Strikes match, lights cigarette.*)

ALMA. —What did I have? (JOHN *stands, holding burning match in his hand. It is a long kitchen match and it makes a good flame. Both stare at it with a sorrowful understanding that is still perplexed.*)

JOHN. You couldn't name it and I couldn't recognize it. I thought it was just a puritanical ice that glittered like flame. But now I believe it *was* flame, mistaken for ice. (ALMA *leans forward and blows out match. He tosses it to floor. Moving away down* L.) I still don't understand it, but I know it was there,—(*Turns to her.*) —just as I know that your eyes and your voice are the two most beautiful things I've ever known—and also the warmest, although they don't seem to be set in your body at all . . . (*Crosses to chair below desk, sits.*)

ALMA. You talk as if my body had ceased to exist for you, John, in spite of the fact that you've just counted my pulse. (*Turns and crosses up* R.) Yes, that's it! (*Turns, faces him, crosses down to* R. *side of desk, clutching it.*) You tried to avoid it, but you've told me plainly. The tables have turned, yes, the tables have turned with a vengeance! You've come around to my old way of thinking and I to yours like two people exchanging a call on each other at the same time, and each one finding the other one gone out, the door locked against him and no one to answer the bell! I came here to tell you that being a gentleman doesn't seem so important to me any more, but you're telling me I've got to remain a lady! (*Violently.*) The tables have turned with a vengeance! (*She recovers control with an obvious effort.*)—The air in here smells of ether—it's making me dizzy. . . .

JOHN. (*Rising, crossing up* R. *to window.*) I'll open a window.

ALMA. Please. (*Crosses down to chair below desk, sits.*)

JOHN. (*Opening window.*) There now.

ALMA. Thank you, that's better. (*Takes bag from desk, opens it.*)

74

Do you remember those little white tablets you gave me? I've used them all up and I'd like to have some more.

JOHN. (Crossing to desk.) I'll write the prescription for you. (Picks up pen and prescription pad, starts to write. NELLIE is in waiting room. They hear her voice.)

NELLIE. Johnny! (They both look up. Then JOHN continues to write. When he has finished, he puts pen back on desk, tears sheet off pad. NELLIE calls again.) Johnny!

ALMA. Someone is waiting in the waiting room, John. One of my vocal pupils. The youngest and prettiest one with the least gift for music. The one that you helped wrap up this handkerchief for me. (She has it in her bag. NELLIE rushes in from off L. with a peal of merry laughter. Rushes up to JOHN and hugs him.)

NELLIE. I've been all over town just shouting, shouting!

JOHN. Shouting what?

NELLIE. Glad tidings! (He looks at ALMA over NELLIE's shoulder.)

JOHN. I thought we weren't going to tell anyone for a while?

NELLIE. I couldn't stop myself! (She wheels about to face ALMA, holding JOHN's arms about her.) Oh, Alma, has he told you?

ALMA. (Quietly.) He didn't need to, Nellie. I guessed . . . from the Christmas card with your two names written on it!

NELLIE. (Runs to ALMA, kneels by her R. side, puts head on ALMA's lap.) So, Alma, you were really the first to know!

ALMA. I'm proud of that, Nellie.

NELLIE. (With her head still down, extends her L. hand.) See on my finger! This was the present I couldn't tell you about!

ALMA. Oh, what a lovely, lovely solitaire! But solitaire is such a wrong name for it. Solitaire means single, and this means two! It's blinding, Nellie! Why, it . . . hurts my eyes! (She fights for control. JOHN catches NELLIE's arm and pulls her to him R. C., keeping her face averted from ALMA.)

JOHN. Excuse her, Miss Alma. Nellie's still such a child.

ALMA. (Rising, turning up to desk, picks up hat and gloves.) I've got to run along now.

JOHN. Don't leave your prescription.

ALMA. (Vaguely.) Oh, yes, where's my prescription?

JOHN. On the desk.

ALMA. (Picks up prescription on desk, turns and moves away L.) I'll take it to the drugstore right away! (NELLIE struggles to free

75

*berself from* JOHN'S *embrace, which keeps her from turning to* ALMA.)
NELLIE. Alma, don't go! Johnny, let go of me, Johnny! You're hugging so tight I can't breathe!
ALMA. (*Down* L.) Good-bye.
NELLIE. Alma! (ALMA *stops.*) Alma, you know you're going to sing at the wedding! (ALMA *rushes out* L.) The very first Sunday in spring!—Which will be Palm Sunday! "The Voice That Breathed O'er Eden." (JOHN *rains kisses on* NELLIE'S *forehead, throat and lips. Lights in office dim out to black.*)

## END OF SCENE

(NOTE: In this blackout JOHN closes window which he had opened previously.)

## PART II

### SCENE 6

*The angel of the fountain. About dusk. Light comes up on angel. Then, gradually, playing lights on the fountain area and on sky cyclorama build up.*
ALMA *appears from* L. *at top of steps* L. *Crosses down steps* L. *and pauses at foot to unwrap a small package. Taking out a pill from the box, she crosses to* R. *of fountain, puts pill in her mouth, bends and drinks at fountain. While she is doing this* A YOUNG MAN, ARCHIE KRAMER, *enters from* L., *in a checked suit and derby. Pauses to look up at angel, then starts down steps* L.; *sees* ALMA. *A train whistle in the distance.* YOUNG MAN *clears his throat. Train whistle is repeated.* ALMA *crosses down to bench and sits,* L. *end.* YOUNG MAN *crosses to* R., *whistling, hands in pockets, looking at* ALMA. *When he gets to* R. *of fountain, he turns and faces her.* ALMA, *pushing up her veil, turns and looks at him. Train whistles again.* YOUNG MAN *smiles at* ALMA, *she turns front, he bends to drink at fountain. As he straightens she speaks in a barely audible voice.*

76

ALMA. The water . . . is . . . cool.

YOUNG MAN. (*Turning to her, eagerly.*) Did you say something?

ALMA. I said the water is cool.

YOUNG MAN. (*His hands in pockets, he crosses slowly to* L. C., *above her, keeping his eyes on her.*) Yes, it sure is, it's nice and cool!

ALMA. It's always cool.

YOUNG MAN. Is it?

ALMA. Yes. Yes, even in summer. It comes from deep underground.

YOUNG MAN. That's what keeps it cool. (*Strolls* R. *to* R. C., *hands still in pockets.*)

ALMA. Glorious Hill is famous for its artesian springs.

YOUNG MAN. I didn't know that. (*Takes hands out of pockets, looks up at fountain, back at* ALMA, *then crosses up to fountain, drinks deeply.*)

ALMA. Are you a stranger in town? (*No reply. She turns quickly to look, sees him still drinking, turns front again.*) Are you a stranger in town?

YOUNG MAN. (*Straightening up from fountain, moving down a step.*) I'm a travelling salesman.

ALMA. Ah, you're a salesman who travels! (*Laughs gently.*) But you're younger than most of them are, and not so fat!

YOUNG MAN. (*Looking down at his figure.*) I'm just starting out. I travel for Red Cross shoes.

ALMA. Ah! The Delta's your territory?

YOUNG MAN. (*Crosses to* L. C., *above bench.*) From the Peabody Lobby to Cat-Fish row in Vicksburg.

ALMA. The life of a travelling salesman is interesting . . . but lonely.

YOUNG MAN. (*Crosses down to* L. *end of bench.*) You're right about that. Hotel bedrooms are lonely. (*Far away the train whistles.*)

ALMA. All rooms are lonely where there is only one person. (*Her eyes fall shut.*)

YOUNG MAN. (*Gently.*) You're tired, aren't you?

ALMA. I? Tired? (*She starts to deny it, then laughs faintly and confesses the truth.*) Yes . . . a little. . . . But I shall rest now. I've just now taken one of my sleeping tablets.

YOUNG MAN. So early?

ALM,ι. Oh, it won't put me to sleep. It will just quiet my nerves.

YOUNG MAN. What are you nervous about?

ALMA. I won an argument this afternoon.

YOUNG MAN. (*Crosses* R. *above bench to down* R.) That's nothing to be nervous over. You ought to be nervous if you lost one.

ALMA. It wasn't the argument that I wanted to win. . . .

YOUNG MAN. Well, I'm nervous, too.

ALMA. What over?

YOUNG MAN. (*Moving up a step and toward her.*) It's my first job and I'm scared of not making good. (*That mysteriously sudden intimacy that sometimes occurs between strangers more completely than old friends or lovers, moves them both.* ALMA *holds out box of tablets to him.*)

ALMA. Then you must take one of my tablets.

YOUNG MAN. Shall I?

ALMA. Please take one!

YOUNG MAN. (*Crosses to her, takes tablet.*) Yes, I shall.

ALMA. You'll be surprised how infinitely merciful they are. (*Holding up box so he can read label.*) The prescription number is 96814. I think of it as the telephone number of God! (*They both laugh. He places one of tablets on his tongue and crosses up to fountain to wash it down.*)

YOUNG MAN. (*After he drinks, looks up at stone figure.*) Thanks, angel. (*Gives her a little salute, then leans on fountain.*)

ALMA. Life is full of little mercies like that, not *big* mercies but comfortable little mercies. And so we go on . . . (*She has leaned back with half-closed eyes.*)

YOUNG MAN. (*Crosses down to her, gently, above* R. *end of bench.*) You're falling asleep.

ALMA. Oh, no, I'm not. I'm just closing my eyes. (*Turns to him.*) You know what I feel like now? I feel like a water-lily.

YOUNG MAN. A water-lily?

ALMA. Yes, I feel like a water-lily on a Chinese lagoon. Won't you sit down? (*He hesitates a moment, removes his hat, crosses down and sits* R. *end of bench, holding his hat awkwardly, looking away from her.*) My name is Alma. Spanish for soul! What's yours?

YOUNG MAN. (*Turning to her.*) Mine's Archie Kramer. (*With a wave of his hand.*) Mucho gusto, as they say in Spain. (*They laugh.*)

ALMA. Usted habla Español, señor?

YOUNG MAN. Un poquito! Usted habla Español, Señorita?

ALMA. Me tambien. Un poquito! (*Laughs.*)

YOUNG MAN. (*Delightedly, laughs.*) Ha . . . ha . . . ha! Sometimes un poquito is plenty. (ALMA *laughs . . . in a way different from the way she has ever laughed before. A little wearily, but quite naturally.* YOUNG MAN *leans toward her confidentially.*) What's there to do in this town after dark?

ALMA. There's not much to do in this town after dark, but there are resorts on the Lake that offer all kinds of after-dark entertainment. There's one called Moon Lake Casino. It's under new management now, but I don't suppose its character has changed.

YOUNG MAN. What was its character?

ALMA. Gay, very gay, Mr. Kramer. . . .

YOUNG MAN. (*Rises, crosses up* C.) Then what in hell are we sitting here for? (*Looks back at her, puts on his hat, comes down a step.*) Vaminos!

ALMA. (*Rises, moves a step toward him.*) Como no, Señor!

YOUNG MAN. I'll call a taxi. (*Running up steps* L.) Taxi! (*As he goes off* L.) Taxi! (*As* ALMA *crosses up to steps,* L., *the grave mood of the play is reinstated with a phrase of music. At foot of steps she faces the stone angel and raises her hand in a sort of valedictory salute. Then turns and starts up steps as . . .*)

## THE CURTAIN FALLS

## END OF PLAY

## PROPERTY LIST

### Part I—Scene 1

Handbag (Alma)
Parasol and handkerchief (Alma)
Firecracker and matches (John)

Small pocket flask (John)
Cigarette and matches (John)
French-horn case (Roger)

### Part I—Scene 2

Palm-leaf fan (Doctor)
Bottles, books, a few simple med-

ical instruments (Doctor)

### Part I—Scene 3

Parasol (Mrs. Winemiller)
Fancy white plumed hat (Mrs. Winemiller)

Jigsaw puzzle (Mrs. Winemiller)
2 glasses—1 with water, 1 with Bromo Seltzer (John)

### Part I—Scene 4

Minute-book with some loose sheets (Alma)
Thick play MS. (Vernon)

Fan (Roger)
Few pages of small MS. (Rosemary)

### Part I—Scene 5

Bandage (John)
Glass half-full of whiskey (Rosemary)
Thermos jug and glass (John)
Bottle with medicine tablets (John)

Watch (John)
Stethoscope (Doctor)
Ring (Alma)
Box of medicine tablets (John)
Anatomy chart (John)

### Part I—Scene 6

MS. paper, pen and ink (Winemiller)
Watch (Winemiller)
Eyeglasses (Winemiller)

Fan (Mrs. Winemiller)
Cigarette and matches (Mrs. Winemiller)
Hat and gloves (Alma)

### Part I—Scene 7

Small table with lamp fastened to it (Dusty)
2 chairs (Dusty)
Matches (Dusty)
Handbag (Alma)

Box of pills (Alma)
Gloves and veil (Alma)
Bottle of wine; 2 glasses (Dusty)
Cigarettes and matches (John)

## PART II—SCENE 1

Pitcher with lemonade, glasses, tray
Photos and post cards (Roger)
Watch (Roger)
Puzzle (Alma)
Bottle of champagne and glass (John)
Revolver (Gonzales)
Roll of bills (Gonzales)
Cane and hat (Dr. Buchanan, Senior)

## PART II—SCENE 2

Tray with coffee things and towel (Alma)

## PART II—SCENE 3

Plumed hat and scarf (Mrs. Winemiller)
Ring (Alma)
Newspaper (Winemiller)
Loving cup (John)
Handkerchief (John)
Book (Nellie)
Paper bag with candy (Nellie)

## PART II—SCENE 4

Fancy baskets with Christmas packages, 1 small one tied with ribbon and with a sprig of holly, with fancy handkerchief and card in it
Pin for holly (Alma)

## PART II—SCENE 5

Stethoscope (John)
Tray with microscope, test-tubes in rack, small medical instruments (John)
Hat, gloves, handbag (Alma)
Ring (Alma)
Cigarette and matches (John)
Prescription pad and pen (John)

## PART II—SCENE 6

Small package in which is pill-box with pills (Alma)

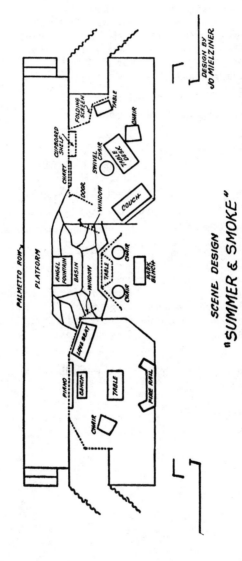

SCENE DESIGN
"SUMMER & SMOKE"

NOTE: DOTTED WALLS OF ROOMS ARE GAUZE OVER OUTLINE PATTERN FRAMES

DESIGN BY
JO MIELZINER

# NEW PLAYS

• **MERE MORTALS** by David Ives, author of *All in the Timing*. Another critically acclaimed evening of one-act comedies combining wit, satire, hilarity and intellect -- a winning combination. The entire evening of plays can be performed by 3 men and 3 women. ISBN: 0-8222-1632-9

• **BALLAD OF YACHIYO** by Philip Kan Gotanda. A provocative play about innocence, passion and betrayal, set against the backdrop of a Hawaiian sugar plantation in the early 1900s. *"Gotanda's writing is superb ... a great deal of fine craftsmanship on display here, and much to enjoy."* --*Variety*. *"...one of the country's most consistently intriguing playwrights..."* --*San Francisco Examiner*. *"As he has in past plays, Gotanda defies expectations..."* --*Oakland Tribune*. [3M, 4W] ISBN: 0-8222-1547-0

• **MINUTES FROM THE BLUE ROUTE** by Tom Donaghy. While packing up a house, a family converges for a weekend of flaring tempers and shattered illusions. *"With MINUTES FROM THE BLUE ROUTE [Donaghy] succeeds not only in telling a story -- a typically American one with wide appeal, about how parents and kids struggle to understand each other and mostly fail -- but in notating it inventively, through wittily elliptical, crisscrossed speeches, and in making it carry a fairly vast amount of serious weight with surprising ease."* --*Village Voice*. [2M, 2W] ISBN: 0-8222-1608-6

• **SCAPIN** by Molière, adapted by Bill Irwin and Mark O'Donnell. This adaptation of Molière's 325-year-old farce, *Les Fourberies de Scapin*, keeps the play in period while adding a late Twentieth Century spin to the language and action. *"This SCAPIN, [with a] felicitous adaptation by Mark O'Donnell, would probably have gone over big with the same audience who first saw Molière's Fourberies de Scapin...in Paris in 1671."* --*N.Y. Times*. *"Commedia dell'arte and vaudeville have at least two things in common: baggy pants and Bill Irwin. All make for a natural fit in the celebrated clown's entirely unconventional adaptation."* --*Variety* [9M, 3W, flexible] ISBN: 0-8222-1603-5

• **THE TURN OF THE SCREW** adapted for the stage by Jeffrey Hatcher from the story by Henry James. The American master's classic tale of possession is given its most interesting "turn" yet: one woman plays the mansion's terrified governess while a single male actor plays everyone else. *"In his thoughtful adaptation of Henry James' spooky tale, Jeffrey Hatcher does away with the supernatural flummery, exchanging the story's balanced ambiguities about the nature of reality for a portrait of psychological vampirism..."* --*Boston Globe*. [1M, 1W] ISBN: 0-8222-1554-3

• **NEVILLE'S ISLAND** by Tim Firth. A middle management orientation exercise turns into an hilarious disaster when the team gets "shipwrecked" on an uninhabited island. *"NEVILLE'S ISLAND ... is that rare event: a genuinely good new play..., it's a comedic, adult LORD OF THE FLIES..."* --*The Guardian*. *"... A non-stop, whitewater deluge of comedy both sophisticated and slapstick.... Firth takes a perfect premise and shoots it to the extreme, flipping his fish out of water, watching them flop around a bit, and then masterminding the inevitable feeding frenzy."* --*New Mexican*. [4M] ISBN: 0-8222-1581-0

**DRAMATISTS PLAY SERVICE, INC.**
440 Park Avenue South, New York, NY 10016  212-683-8960  Fax 212-213-1539
postmaster@dramatists.com  www.dramatists.com

# NEW PLAYS

• **TAKING SIDES by Ronald Harwood.** Based on the true story of one of the world's greatest conductors whose wartime decision to remain in Germany brought him under the scrutiny of a U.S. Army determined to prove him a Nazi. *"A brave, wise and deeply moving play delineating the confrontation between culture, and power, between art and politics, between irresponsible freedom and responsible compromise."* --London Sunday Times. [4M, 3W] ISBN: 0-8222-1566-7

• **MISSING/KISSING by John Patrick Shanley.** Two biting short comedies, MISSING MARISA and KISSING CHRISTINE, by one of America's foremost dramatists and the Academy Award winning author of *Moonstruck*. *" ... Shanley has an unusual talent for situations ... and a sure gift for a kind of inner dialogue in which people talk their hearts as well as their minds...."* --N.Y. Post. MISSING MARISA [2M], KISSING CHRISTINE [1M, 2W] ISBN: 0-8222-1590-X

• **THE SISTERS ROSENSWEIG by Wendy Wasserstein, Pulitzer Prize-winning author of *The Heidi Chronicles*.** Winner of the 1993 Outer Critics Circle Award for Best Broadway Play. A captivating portrait of three disparate sisters reuniting after a lengthy separation on the eldest's 50th birthday. *"The laughter is all but continuous."* --New Yorker. *"Funny. Observant. A play with wit as well as acumen.... In dealing with social and cultural paradoxes, Ms. Wasserstein is, as always, the most astute of commentators."* --N.Y. Times. [4M, 4W] ISBN: 0-8222-1348-6

• **MASTER CLASS by Terrence McNally. Winner of the 1996 Tony Award for Best Play.** Only a year after winning the Tony Award for *Love! Valour! Compassion!*, Terrence McNally scores again with the most celebrated play of the year, an unforgettable portrait of Maria Callas, our century's greatest opera diva. *"One of the white-hot moments of contemporary theatre. A total triumph."* --N.Y. Post. *"Blazingly theatrical."* -- USA Today. [3M, 3W] ISBN: 0-8222-1521-7

• **DEALER'S CHOICE by Patrick Marber.** A weekly poker game pits a son addicted to gambling against his own father, who also has a problem but won't admit it. *"... make tracks to DEALER'S CHOICE, Patrick Marber's wonderfully masculine, razor-sharp dissection of poker-as-life.... It's a play that comes out swinging and never lets up -- a witty, wisecracking drama that relentlessly probes the tortured souls of its six very distinctive ... characters. CHOICE is a cutthroat pleasure that you won't want to miss."* --Time Out (New York). [6M] ISBN: 0-8222-1616-7

• **RIFF RAFF by Laurence Fishburne.** RIFF RAFF marks the playwriting debut of one of Hollywood's most exciting and versatile actors. *"Mr. Fishburne is surprisingly and effectively understated, with scalding bubbles of anxiety breaking through the surface of a numbed calm."* --N.Y. Times. *"Fishburne has a talent and a quality...[he] possesses one of the vital requirements of a playwright -- a good ear for the things people say and the way they say them."* --N.Y. Post. [3M] ISBN: 0-8222-1545-4

DRAMATISTS PLAY SERVICE, INC.
440 Park Avenue South, New York, NY 10016 212-683-8960 Fax 212-213-1539
postmaster@dramatists.com www.dramatists.com